BIRDS OF PREY

ACKNOWLEDGMENTS

The author and publishers would like to thank the following for their help in the compilation of this book:
The National Museums of Scotland, Edinburgh: Andrew Kitchener and David Heppell of the Department of Natural History; the former Head of Library, Manjil V. Mathew and his staff. The Natural History Museum, London: the Head of Library Services, Rex Banks and his staff. The Linnean Society of London: the Council and Librarian, Gina Douglas. Henry Sotheran Limited, Antiquarian Booksellers, London: the Print Department. The Zoological Society of London: the Librarian, R A. Fish. Ken Smith Photography (Edinburgh). Cavendish House, Carlisle: Una Dance, Robert Dance.

They would also like to thank the following for their kind permission to photograph the original prints in their possession:
The National Museums of Scotland, Edinburgh for the plates appearing on pages 21, 27, 33, 39, 41, 47, 49, 59, 61, 63, 65, 67, 69, 71, 93, 107, 119, 121 and 125. Henry Sotheran Limited, London for the plates appearing on pages 9, 15, 17, 23, 29, 35, 43, 45, 51, 55, 73, 75, 77, 81, 89, 103, 109, 117 and 127. The Zoological Society of London for the plates appearing on pages 11, 13, 19, 25, 31, 37, 53, 57, 79, 85, 87, 91, 95, 97, 99, 101, 105, 111, 113 and 123. The Natural History Museum, London for the plates appearing on pages 83 and 115.

Classic Natural History Prints, *Birds of Prey*
published in 1991 by Studio Editions Ltd.
Princess House, 50 Eastcastle Street
London W1N 7AP, England

Printed and bound in Italy

ISBN 1 85170 629 1

CLASSIC NATURAL HISTORY PRINTS

BIRDS OF PREY

BY JOSEPH WOLF

S. PETER DANCE

STUDIO EDITIONS
LONDON

INTRODUCTION   5

LIST OF PLATES

INDEX   128

INTRODUCTION

"Without exception the best all-round animal painter that ever lived." So said Sir Edwin Landseer when speaking of Joseph Wolf to Henry E. Dresser, a prominent figure in British and European ornithology. As Landseer's own reputation as an animal painter stood very high in Britain – for most Victorians his "Monarch of the glen" represented the pinnacle of animal art – this was high praise. Landseer's comment will not seem extravagant to connoisseurs of that art, especially of the exacting branch of it devoted to bird portraiture, but it will be meaningless to those unacquainted with Wolf's work. Even in Wolf's lifetime only a cultured few would have known who Landseer was talking about.

One of the purposes of this book, therefore, is to introduce an outstanding animal painter – he would now be called a wildlife artist – to a wider audience and to highlight his achievements in one specialized department of animal art: the portrayal of birds of prey. Another is to say something about the birds shown in the plates reproduced here. In Wolf's day little was known about many of the species he illustrated, but much more is known about most of them now. Conversely, a great deal that was written about some species then has been largely forgotten or overlooked since. This is a good opportunity to recall, often in direct quotation, what some of Wolf's contemporaries and precursors said about them.

Joseph Wolf was born on 21 January 1820, the eldest son of Anton Wolf, Headman of the village of Mörz in the valley of the River Moselle. Distant some fifteen miles from the city of Koblenz and two miles from the market town of Münstermaifeld, the village was surrounded by woods, fields and streams which provided wildlife in great variety. As a boy, Joseph learned how to trap mammals; as a youth, how to handle a gun. He took every opportunity to explore the countryside around him, observed the local fauna and flora and discovered the joys of solitude among natural surroundings. For someone disposed to study natural history, his was an ideal situation.

He would often sketch the creatures he shot or whose movements he observed, some of his sketches showing a remarkable artistic precocity for one so young and untaught. He made a good set of paintbrushes by taking the longer, elastic hairs from the tails of Beech Martens and tying them into quills taken from crows and thrushes. Predatory birds, he discovered, fascinated him more than any other forms of wildlife and he was well placed to observe and draw them. One of his earliest sketches was of a captive Eagle Owl he had seen in a hotel yard at Münstermaifeld; and Goshawks preying upon poultry or pigeons often fell victim to his gun and provided him with excellent subjects. Living in a district on the route of many birds of passage, he became acquainted with Red Kites and Black Kites flying south-west as the weather became more congenial. Occasionally a Honey Buzzard would put in an appearance; and he soon took for granted the sight of Merlins, Hobbies, Sparrowhawks and Kestrels. He became adept at catching some of these birds with spring-traps of his own invention and so was able to make sketches of living models at close range.

In this way, alone and without encouragement, he laid the foundation of his profound knowledge of birds, knowledge which was to stand him in good stead throughout his future career. Disliking farm work, he thought he would seek the training which would enable him to become a painter of birds. But first he had to earn a living, if possible in a way congenial to his interests. He decided to look for work as a lithographer, one who drew pictures on smooth blocks of limestone from which

A PEREGRINE TIERCEL. A PRELIMINARY STUDY IN CHARCOAL, DRAWN IN 1876.

prints could be obtained and then coloured by hand. Lithography, the process which produced the original versions of all the prints reproduced in this book, was flourishing then and provided employment in many German cities.

At first Anton Wolf, who could not understand his son's desire to be a lithographer, nor his passion for natural history and art, opposed his repeated requests to leave home, but finally he agreed to let him go. Meanwhile Joseph had found some solace in making miniature sketches of birds in water-colours, exquisite studies correct to the last detail. In his old age he explained their small scale by saying that he could not cover a large space to his satisfaction. Finding employment as a lithographer locally proved to be difficult and unremunerative, so he went to Frankfurt and there met Eduard Rüppell, who was impressed by the young man's sketches and promised him work. This led to Wolf being commissioned to illustrate a volume on the birds of north-eastern Africa for Rüppell, his first substantial commission. Thus, in his early twenties, he began the career that was to sustain him for the rest of his life and, to some extent, was to bring him fame.

He went to Darmstadt, where he helped Johann J. Kaup to set up a stuffed Sparrowhawk for his museum and showed the distinguished ornithologist his sketches of birds. Kaup took Wolf's sketch-book with him to Leiden and showed it to another eminent ornithologist, Professor Hermann Schlegel. The sketches of predatory birds so impressed Schlegel that he asked the young man to send him some life-size drawings of Goshawks, adult and young. When they arrived, Schlegel was so pleased with them that he commissioned Wolf to illustrate an ambitious folio work about falconry he was writing with A.H. Verster van Wulverhorst, the *Traité de Fauconnerie*. The lithographed plates based on Wolf's designs appeared in the 1840s and these assured him a reputation as a bird artist of rare talent. At their best they are superb, the shortcomings of the lesser ones being attributable mostly to the rigid poses of the stuffed birds the artist sometimes used as his models.

Wolf spent about four years at Darmstadt fulfilling other commissions. The most important of these was for twenty lithographs to illustrate a volume on Japanese birds, one of a series of volumes describing and illustrating the fauna of Japan, edited by Philipp F. von Siebold. This must have been a difficult commission for Wolf because most of the birds were unknown to him and were probably poorly preserved.

Sometimes he would spend a day shooting game with an old Darmstadt sportsman who had befriended him. At the day's end he would make diagrams of the birds he had bagged, showing outlines of head and feet and the exact positions, shapes and areas of the various tracts of feathers, with additional sketches showing the shapes and markings of individual feathers. More than a century later, when Charles F. Tunnicliffe's "measured drawings" of birds came up for sale at auction in London, the importance to a bird artist of such exercises was made obvious. Few who saw Tunnicliffe's drawings then could have known about Joseph Wolf's much earlier use of similar pictorial references. At Darmstadt, too, he began to master the drawings of trees and foliage, gnarled trunks, peeling bark, broken boughs and other features which were later to be such conspicuous elements of his foregrounds. He knew that the beauty of mammals and birds could be greatly enhanced by the intricate shapes and the varied colouring of their environments; and he had been very disappointed with the scenic "accessories" added by another lithographer to the plates he had prepared for the *Traité de Fauconnerie*.

Darmstadt had been very beneficial for him. So had Dr Kaup. It was he who now introduced Wolf by name to the publisher John Gould, then a comparative newcomer to ornithological and publishing circles in high-Victorian Britain. Gould sent Wolf a commission for a small water-colour drawing of birds and so initiated an uneasy but important alliance between the two. At the British Museum, Dr Kaup was asked about the artist who had drawn the falcons illustrated in the *Traité de Fauconnerie* and this led to another commission: to complete the illustrations for George R. Gray's *The Genera of Birds* . Wolf declined to take up this commission immediately because he wanted to complete some formal art training at Antwerp. But the die was cast. London and all it could offer to a young and ambitious artist now beckoned him.

He arrived there in February 1848 and at once started work at the British Museum, fulfilling the commission he had turned down so recently. At the age of twenty-eight the farmer's boy with a penchant for natural history and art who used brushes made from the tails of wild animals he had shot himself, was installed – if only temporarily – at an important institution in one of the great centres of learning. Except for excursions to places of natural history interest, Joseph Wolf, as the celebrated animal artist with a liking for expensive cigars who – eventually – could afford to furnish his own studio, was to have a London address for the rest of his life.

Throughout the middle years of the nineteenth century London was a good place to be if you were an animal artist, especially if you understood the art of "drawing on the stone",

for there was plenty of work available making lithographic designs for publishers. At first, however, Wolf had ambitions as a painter and by 1849 he had made sufficient progress to have his work exhibited at the Royal Academy. Most of his pictures received unfavourable notices from establishment art critics who could not accept the validity of compositions based on faithful observations of nature. Some other qualified judges of art, however, had a more generous opinion of his artistic abilities. A.H. Palmer, who published a doting biography of Wolf in 1895, wrote to Thomas Woolner, one of the original members of the Pre-Raphaelite Brotherhood, who replied, "I cannot speak in words of Wolf as highly as he deserves, and I am rejoiced that you seem resolved to do his splendid abilities justice. I remember fighting his battles as far back as 1848, when many persons were inclined to disallow his high originality and vivid truthfulness; and I doubt, even now, if there are a great number who appreciate his works as they ought to be admired." When Wolf became better known, however, he was often asked for oil paintings of animals in naturalistic settings to decorate the homes of wealthy landowners, politicians and businessmen.

Some prominent members of society were happy to make his acquaintance. Lord Derby, a great collector of mammals and birds, alive or dead, invited Wolf to visit his remarkable menagerie and museum at Knowsley, near Liverpool, and he stayed there for two profitable months. Gould tracked him down early and the two of them stayed with the Duke of Westminster in west Sutherland, where Wolf observed the Golden Eagle. Lord Tweedmouth invited him to Inverness-shire to study the Osprey and commissioned him to paint six huge panels in oils. He was happy to accept such commissions, delighted when they gave him an opportunity to observe birds in the wild, enraptured when they took him to Scotland, the home then of some of his favourite birds of prey. The Zoological Gardens in Regent's Park, however, were a constant source of pleasure and inspiration, as they had been to the youthful Edward Lear before him. Here, in the heart of London, he could observe and sketch exotic birds and other animals at any time.

But his earnings as a creative artist working in oils or water-colours were unreliable and insufficient to meet his living expenses. He needed bread-and-butter money. This he continued to obtain by involving himself in the production of lithographic prints to illustrate the literature of natural history, especially of ornithology. Most of these prints appeared in scientific books and journals. Sometimes he drew directly on to the stone but, as his reputation grew, he usually drew on paper and the responsibility for transferring his drawings on to the stone surface devolved upon others. What we then see is someone else's transcription of his original artwork. Fortunately he was well served by most of those who lithographed and coloured the final prints.

Ironically he is now best known by the work he did for John Gould, the publisher whose folio-size lithographs of birds have been peddled enthusiastically by print-sellers for many years, either in their original form or as cheap reproductions. Gould, or rather the artists and colourists working under his direction, usually succeeded in making birds look very attractive, which is why so many of them have ended up, mounted and framed, on the walls of suburban bedrooms and cosmopolitan hotels. Regrettably he had no eye for composition, did not know or seemed not to know what birds looked like in the wild but was satisfied to show them in tame poses and could not resist the temptation to heighten their natural colouring. The birds in the prints he published look pretty because he knew that prettiness was the quality likely to make prospective purchasers part with their money. He was a good businessman but an overbearing employer who stopped at nothing to get what he wanted.

Unfortunately Wolf did not share Gould's liking for prettiness in bird pictures and he did not think much of him as a person either. Gould had rapidly acquired a formidable reputation, however, and was already known to many as "The Bird Man". As a successful publisher of bird books he could have provided steady employment for a gifted bird artist, but Wolf usually declined his repeated offers of work. Gould was not easily deterred, however, and could be persuasive, producing a tempting cigar while asking Wolf to make a charcoal sketch of a bird for him or praising his artistic abilities. Most of all Gould wanted Wolf to work with him on *The Birds of Great Britain*, the book many regard as his finest publishing achievement. Wolf agreed to contribute water-colour drawings of about fifty-five species to the project. Nearly half of these were birds of prey and this subject-matter may explain Wolf's acquiescence. By general consent the lithographs made from them are among the best ever published by Gould. To Wolf, however, most of the hand-coloured prints were vulgarized, over-coloured versions of his originals.

Wolf had a very different, entirely satisfactory, working arrangement with his friend Henry E. Dresser, whose multi-volume *A History of the Birds of Europe* was for many years the standard work on the subject. He provided drawings in grey charcoal (a favourite medium of his) for fifteen of the lithographs contained in it, among them those showing the various harriers. The illustrations of these birds in Dresser's treatise are usually not so highly coloured as those in Gould's *The Birds of Great Britain*.

Less glamorous but more truthful were the many lithographs of birds Wolf contributed to the *Transactions of the Zoological Society of London* and the ornithological journal *Ibis*. The birds were always shown as though they had been drawn from life, a deception made possible by Wolf's profound knowledge of bird structure and behaviour, for his models were usually museum specimens. As little was known about most of the species he portrayed – many of them were new to science when he drew them – it is remarkable that his reconstructions of their probable appearance in life are so accurate.

As a London-based animal artist, Joseph Wolf lived a busy but contented life, fulfilling his many commissions, visiting the Zoological Gardens, entertaining fellow artists and naturalists or attending to the birds in his aviaries at home. He died in 1899, leaving behind him many original oil-paintings, water-colours and charcoal sketches. It is by these artworks that he would have preferred posterity to judge him, but they are now widely dispersed and seldom exhibited to a wide audience. Hand-coloured Victorian lithographs are all that most of us ever see of his art, although many of these are brilliantly conceived and pleasing to the eye.

The prints selected for reproduction here all show birds of prey. Gyrfalcon, Hobby, Merlin, Snowy Owl and many more besides, they comprise a gallery of Joseph Wolf's favourite subjects, an enduring legacy of "the best all-round animal painter that ever lived".

JOSEPH WOLF IN THE FIFTIES. FROM A.H. PALMER'S LIFE OF JOSEPH WOLF, 1895.

Black Kite (1872)

BLACK KITE, *Milvus migrans*. Hand–coloured lithograph by W. Hart from an original drawing by J. Wolf, pl. 23 (in Part 22, 1872) from Vol. 1 of J. Gould's *The Birds of Great Britain*, 1862–73. Size of plate 21¾″ × 14½″.

The Black Kite is a migratory bird found throughout most of Europe and Asia, much of Africa and the northern parts of Australasia and this helps explain the variation in its appearance. There are distinct differences in the intensity of colour and in the shape of the tail. In Asian and African specimens the tail is more forked than it is in specimens from Europe (although the tail of the Red Kite, *Milvus milvus*, is more forked than that of any Black Kite). Wolf's picture was probably based on a skin or a stuffed specimen of the form prevalent in western Europe, but Gould's text is silent on this point. Up to the time when this print was published only one example had ever been shot in Britain and there is nothing to suggest it was the one Wolf used as his model.

In some parts of the world the Black Kite is extraordinarily abundant and is often reckless when after food. Gould quotes some comments published in 1865 by Henry Baker Tristram, who had watched its antics in the Holy Land: "The Black Kite, never once seen in winter, returns in immense numbers from the south, and about the beginning of March scatters itself over the whole country, preferring especially the neighbourhood of villages, where it is a welcome and unmolested guest, and certainly does not appear to attack the poultry, among which it may often be seen feeding on garbage. It is not strictly gregarious, though very sociable; and the slaughter of a sheep near the tents will soon attract a large party of Kites, which swoop down, regardless of man and guns, and enjoy a noisy scramble for the refuse, chasing each other in a laughable fashion, and sometimes enabling the wily Raven to steal off with the coveted morsel during their contention."

MILVUS MIGRANS, Bodd.

J.Wolf & W.Hart, del et lith.   Walter, Imp

Black Kite (1844)

LE MILAN À OREILLES NOIRES, *Milvus melanotis* (now Black Kite, *Milvus migrans*). Hand-coloured lithograph by J. Wolf, pl. 5 (1844) from P.F. von Siebold's *Fauna Japonica, Description des Oiseaux*, 1844–50. Size of plate 15½" × 11".

This is one of several illustrations Wolf prepared for the *Fauna Japonica*, an ambitious but unfinished work edited by Philipp Franz von Siebold and written by others, among them the Dutch ornithologist Hermann Schlegel, co-author of a magnificent folio treatise on falconry which was mostly illustrated from original drawings by Wolf. The lithographs of birds of prey Wolf contributed to the *Fauna Japonica* may all have been made from drawings of preserved skins. The skins would probably have been less than pristine by the time they reached Europe and Wolf would have had some difficulty trying to portray them in lifelike postures. This explains why they do not have the impact of some of his other bird portraits.

There are many forms, or subspecies of this bird, the one illustrated here being an adult male of the form occurring in Japan and elsewhere in the Far East. Distributed over a large part of the Old World and Australasia, the Black Kite in one or other of its guises is one of the most successful birds of prey of its size anywhere. It is a well-known bird on the plains of northern India and Kashmir, but it is also a familiar sight in the Himalayas at altitudes up to about eight thousand feet.

$\frac{1}{2}$

Govinda Kite (1852)

GOVINDA KITE, *Milvus govinda* (now *Milvus migrans govinda*). Hand-coloured lithograph by H.C. Richter from an original drawing by J. Wolf, pl. 11 (in Part 4, 1852) from Vol. 1 of J. Gould's *The Birds of Asia*, 1849–83. Size of plate 21½″ × 14½″.

Gould was indebted to a Captain Boys for the specimens upon which Wolf based his drawing of the Govinda Kite, now considered to be a form of the Black Kite. Captain Boys was one of that large band of British military personnel who turned to natural history pursuits during their long tours of duty in India. From such men Gould obtained important information about exotic birds. He also relied on information published by other ornithologists, among them Thomas Claverhill Jerdon, author of a two-volume book about Indian birds.

Gould drew upon Jerdon's book and other sources for information about the so-called Govinda Kite. Jerdon says that this "very useful bird" was plentiful, especially in the cantonments, camps and villages, and it was always looking out for refuse of all kinds. According to a Colonel Sykes, this bird was constantly soaring in circles watching for an opportunity to dart down upon a chicken or upon animal refuse thrown from the cook-room; and occasionally it would even stoop at a dish of meat being carried from the cook-room to the house. Out in the country it preyed chiefly upon reptiles and was remarkably fond of fish. From another source Gould discovered that this otherwise attractive bird was usually very smelly and swarmed with lice.

Red Kite (1868)

KITE, *Milvus regalis* (now Red Kite, *Milvus milvus*). Hand-coloured lithograph by H.C. Richter from an original drawing by J. Wolf, pl. 22 (in Part 13, 1868) from Vol. 1 of J. Gould's *The Birds of Great Britain*, 1862–73. Size of plate 21¾″ × 14½″.

The Red Kite has a much more restricted range than the Black Kite, occurring only in western Europe, Asia Minor and north-west Africa. It is still often seen around built-up areas in the Canary Islands and the Cape Verde group. In Shakespeare's day it was a common sight in London, where its scavenging propensities were considered so beneficial that killing it was forbidden. Visitors to the metropolis expressed surprise at its number and familiarity. "They have been called 'docile birds'", says Gould, speaking of kites generally, "because it is the nature of some, if not all the species, to sit about on the branches of trees near cities, villages, cantonments, and farm-steads, and thence to make forays into the very streets, and sometimes to become so bold as to suddenly descend and clutch the passing joint while being carried from the kitchen to the house or tent."

It usually builds its nest in the fork of a large tree and will incorporate into it a motley collection of bits and pieces. Gould refers to a description of an old nest found in Huntingdonshire which was lined with "small pieces of linen, part of a saddle-girth, a bit of a harvest-glove, part of a straw bonnet, pieces of paper, and a worsted garter; and in the midst of this singular collection of materials were deposited two eggs."

MILVUS REGALIS.

J. Wolf & H.C.Richter, del. et lith.

Walter Imp.

Northern Goshawk (1869)

GOSHAWK, *Astur palumbarius* (now Northern Goshawk, *Accipiter gentilis*). Hand-coloured lithograph by H.C. Richter from an original drawing by J. Wolf, pl. 9 (in Part 15, 1869) from Vol. 1 of J. Gould's *The Birds of Great Britain*, 1862–73. Size of plate 21¾″ × 14½″.

The Northern Goshawk, which ranges across most of the northern hemisphere, is one of the world's largest goshawks, with a maximum height of about twenty-four inches. It sits motionless for hours at a time in the canopy of a leafy tree whence it dashes swiftly through trees, wings partly folded, in pursuit of its prey, which is usually a wild bird or a mammal but occasionally a domestic fowl. Wolf told Gould that he had known it, when pressed by hunger, to dash out of its retreat and give chase to a Short-eared Owl.

Gould says that one of the finest examples of this bird he had ever seen had been shot on a Suffolk estate in 1859. An immature female, the lengthened lanceolate markings on its breast were particularly pleasing to him. "It had been in the neighbourhood for some time previously," he says, "and the keeper had more than once shot at and slightly wounded it; notwithstanding it did not become shy, but evinced a degree of intrepidity very unusual among birds of prey, almost daily leaving the woods and flying skulkingly up the lanes to the farm steadings, just overtopping the buildings, and pouncing down upon a hen or poult as opportunity served – the great scurry, consternation, and cackling of the mother hens bringing the house-wife to the door just in time to see one of her feathered charges taken over the wall: once too often, however, was the foray made; for the keeper was in waiting and shot the culprit."

ASTUR PALUMBARIUS.

J. Wolf & H.C.Richter del et lith.   Walter Imp.

Northern Goshawk (c. 1844)

LE TIERCELET (immature male of the Northern Goshawk, *Accipiter gentilis*). Hand-coloured lithograph by J. Wolf, with additional details by C. Scheuren, pl. 11 (c. 1844) from H. Schlegel and A.H. Verster van Wulverhorst's *Traité de Fauconnerie*, 1844–53. Size of plate 26½″ × 19½″.

As the Netherlands were for long the centre of European falconry, it is not surprising that two Dutchmen should have published the most impressive of all books on the subject. What makes it impressive, of course, are Wolf's life-size illustrations. This is one of the dozen lithographs he executed for Schlegel and Wulverhorst's *Traité de Fauconnerie*. It portrays a male bird, whose vertically disposed markings on its breast show that it is immature. These are the kind of markings, mentioned in the description of the previous plate, which so pleased John Gould, who says that "in no one member of the great family of falcons does there occur a greater dissimilarity between the young bird of the year, with the lanceolate markings of its breast, and the fully adult, in which the same part is crossed by numerous fine bars."

The ancient craft of falconry developed in the Old World, but the sport is now being practised with great enthusiasm and ingenuity in North America. There they now take advantage of the Northern Goshawk's natural hunting tendencies by training it to pursue birds and mammals in wooded environments. To help them find it and its prey after a strike they attach a bell to its legs.

Drawn from ... WOLF .... Published ... WALTER Imp .... London.

LE ... ...

Semicollared Hawk (1860)

ACCIPITER COLLARIS (Semicollared Hawk). Hand-coloured lithograph by J. Wolf, pl. 6 from *Ibis*, Vol. 2, 1860, illustrating an article by P.L. Sclater, "On an undescribed species of Hawk from New Granada". Size of plate 8½″ × 5″.

"The mountain valleys of New Granada – so fertile in zoological novelties of every sort – have produced several birds of prey which are not known to occur elsewhere." So said Philip Lutley Sclater, a leading authority on birds and mammals, when describing the Semicollared Hawk as new to science in 1860. His description of this twelve-inch-long bird appeared in *Ibis*, accompanied by this lithograph, one of many Wolf contributed to that important ornithological journal. The foreground figure was based upon a specimen received by the British Museum in 1854, that in the background being drawn from one in the private collection of J.H. Gurney. "To the same gentleman's liberality", says Sclater, "I am indebted for the plate illustrating this species, from the pencil of Mr. Wolf." Each bird had originated from Bogota, although the species is now known to occur in Ecuador, Venezuela and Colombia. This was not the only occasion when Wolf had to use his artistry and ingenuity to portray in the same picture apparently living examples of birds obtained in a lifeless condition from different sources.

The Semicollared Hawk, like so many of the birds Wolf was commissioned to draw, was known to him only from skins and he had to try to reconstruct its probable appearance in life. It is not surprising that this lover of birds in their natural surroundings, this supreme observer and delineator of living birds, soon tired of such work and continued it only because he needed the money. Under the circumstances it is remarkable that he was able to achieve such satisfying results with such unpromising materials.

Ibis 1860 Pl. VI

ACCIPITER COLLARIS

$\dfrac{1}{2}$

Eurasian Sparrowhawk (1864)

SPARROWHAWK, *Accipiter nisus* (now Eurasian Sparrowhawk). Hand-coloured lithograph by H.C. Richter from an original drawing by J. Wolf, pl. 10 (in Part 5, 1864) from Vol. 1 of J. Gould's *The Birds of Great Britain*, 1862–73. Size of plate 21¾″ × 14½″.

Smaller and more acrobatic than the Northern Goshawk, the Eurasian Sparrowhawk is a woodland bird widely distributed in Europe, Asia and Japan. It is resident in temperate parts of Europe but is mostly a migrant in other parts of its range. Its short, broad wings and long tail enable it to move easily and rapidly among trees, where it surprises and chases songbirds and small mammals. The female – larger and more formidable than the male – has been known to kill leverets and young rabbits. In Wolf's picture the bird in the background is an old female shown in the act of seizing a sparrow from an ivy-covered garden wall. An adult male dominates the foreground.

Having compared the savage and cunning behaviour of this bird with that of the comparatively harmless Old World Kestrel, *Falco tinnunculus*, Gould says, "How varied are the actions and economy of the two birds! How different are they in temper and disposition – one naturally tame and docile, the other morose, sulky, and spiteful, throwing forward its long legs and grasping anything within its reach with its sharp and powerful talons. The very eye of the Sparrow-hawk, beautifully coloured as it is, is indicative of his wicked disposition, while the soft, full black eye of the Kestrel betokens a very different nature." Gould also says he has heard of "a Sparrow-hawk pursuing a Finch between the legs of a man, where it had flown for shelter; and in the course of my life I have known many instances of its dashing through or killing itself against a pane of glass in pursuit of a bird, or when flying at a caged bird within." His comments help to explain the Eurasian Sparrowhawk's popularity among falconers.

J. Wolf and H.C.Richter, del. & lith.

ACCIPITER NISIS.

Walter & Cohn, Imp.

Japanese Lesser Sparrowhawk (1844)

L'ÉPERVIER À GORGE RAYÉ, *Astur (Nisus) gularis* (now Japanese Lesser Sparrowhawk, *Accipiter gularis*). Hand-coloured lithograph by J. Wolf, pl. 2 (1844) from P.F. von Siebold's *Fauna Japonica, Description des Oiseaux*, 1844–50. Size of plate 15½″ × 11″.

There are several different sparrowhawks in the Old World, the one shown here being native to woodlands or forests in low-lying districts of Japan, western China, Korea and Manchuria. The Japanese Lesser Sparrowhawk spends the winter months in Burma and Malaya, making its pilgrimages so punctually every year that Chinese falconers know exactly when to capture it on the wing. Like the Old World Kestrel, this ten-inch-long bird has been trained for falconry, but is too small to kill birds larger than a thrush.

This picture shows the contrast between the pale amber-brown breast of the male and the barred rufous-brown and white breast of the female, but in other respects it does not do full justice to the Japanese Lesser Sparrowhawk. Artistically it is not in the same class as the bird portraits Wolf contributed to the *Traité de Fauconnerie*.

ASTUR (NISUS) GULARIS .

Zone-tailed Hawk (1859)

BUTEO ZONOCERCUS (now Zone-tailed Hawk, *Buteo albonotatus*). Hand-coloured lithograph by J. Wolf, pl. 59 (1859) from *Transactions of the Zoological Society of London*, Vol. 4, 1851–62, illustrating P.L. Sclater's article "On some new or little-known species of Accipitres, in the collection of the Norwich Museum". Size of plate 12″ × 9″.

Before Philip Lutley Sclater published the description of *Buteo zonocercus*, a supposedly new species of hawk from Guatemala, G. R. Gray, an ornithologist at the British Museum, had pointed out its similarity to *Buteo albonotatus*, a species described by Gray himself some years earlier. Gray was right and the scientific name Sclater gave to the Zone-tailed Hawk is now forgotten. The picture which accompanied Sclater's description, however, deserves a better fate, for it is a convincingly lifelike representation of a bird which was available to Wolf only in a preserved state. If Wolf could have seen this attractive bird alive in its native haunts he would have marvelled at the way it courses back and forth above the trees, scarcely flapping its wings before plunging falcon-like after its prey. To witness this behaviour he would have had to journey to north-western South America, Mexico or the south-western United States.

During the nineteenth century, however, taking a serious interest in the Zone-tailed Hawk in the United States could be risky, as a certain Captain Bendire discovered. He had climbed a tree to remove the eggs from the nest of one of these birds when he spied a group of Apache warriors looking up at him from a short distance away. He stuffed one of the eggs into his mouth, shinned down the tree, mounted his horse and rode off at top speed to his camp several miles away. He reached camp with the egg intact. Extracting it from his mouth, he discovered, was very painful.

$\frac{1}{2}$

BUTEO SCHLEGELII.

Common Buzzard (1863)

COMMON BUZZARD, *Buteo vulgaris* (now *Buteo buteo*). Hand-coloured lithograph by H.C. Richter from an original drawing by J. Wolf, pl. 6 (in Part 4, 1863) from Vol. 1 of J. Gould's *The Birds of Great Britain*, 1862–73. Size of plate 21¾″ × 14½″.

Nineteenth-century bird artists, especially those commissioned to illustrate books, often had to work from skins or mounted specimens preserved in museums or private collections. This was usually the case with birds of prey, except for those used in falconry, because they were difficult to capture and keep alive. Fortunately for Wolf, who much preferred to make careful drawings of living birds, the Common Buzzard is easy to capture and to maintain in captivity. When Gould needed illustrations of the Common Buzzard he obtained permission from a friend living at Taplow, by the River Thames, for Wolf to make drawings of the finest pair Gould had ever seen, though they had been kept in a large cage for three or four years. This lithograph resulted from Wolf's studies of those two birds. The figure in the background was drawn from a dark-coloured bird killed elsewhere.

The Common Buzzard may be seen today in many parts of Europe and Asia, from the British Isles to China and Japan. In Gould's day it had been so persecuted by gamekeepers and others that he says "it may almost be considered as a bird of the past." He had twice seen it sailing over woods in Cornwall, but he suspected that the birds were only chance visitors there, "for the keeper was alert", he says, "and intended a closer acquaintance the first spare moment he had to devote to them". The Common Buzzard has had more to put up with than over-zealous gamekeepers since Gould's day, but it is now once again a familiar sight in the British Isles, soaring high over moor and mountain or squatting on a fence post. It seems that this bird of the past has a future after all.

BUTEO VULGARIS.

Upland Buzzard (1844)

LA BUSE DEMI-PATTUE, *Buteo hemilasius* (now Upland Buzzard). Hand-coloured lithograph by J. Wolf, pl. 7 (1844) from P.F. von Siebold's *Fauna Japonica, Description des Oiseaux*, 1844–50. Size of plate 15½″ × 11″.

The breeding range of the Upland Buzzard is Tibet and China, but migrant birds are seen in northern India, Burma and Korea. At home in the desert, the open plain or the mountains, it breeds at altitudes between twelve thousand and fifteen thousand feet. Its inclusion in Siebold's *Fauna Japonica* constitutes the only record – an unconvincing one, surely – of this large buzzard for Japan. The older literature dealing with the distribution of birds and other animals is punctuated with doubtful records of this sort, and specialists analyse them carefully before accepting their validity.

With a body length of more than two feet, the Upland Buzzard is as big as a fair-size eagle and must be an impressive sight when soaring among its mountain fastnesses. Although it flies well, it will perch for hours on a rock or some other prominence waiting to pounce on its prey, usually a small mammal. The Chinese, who have no difficulty catching it when it is migrating, use it as a decoy for other hawks. The older nestlings sometimes kill the younger ones and are occasionally guilty of cannibalism.

$\frac{1}{2}$.

Madagascar Buzzard (1862)

MADAGASCAR BUZZARD, *Buteo brachypterus*. Hand-coloured lithograph by J. Wolf, pl. 8 from *Ibis*, Vol. 4, 1862, illustrating an article by S. Roch and E. Newton, "Notes on birds observed in Madagascar". Size of plate 8½″ × 5″.

Next to the Black Kite, *Milvus migrans*, the bird shown here is the commonest predatory bird in Madagascar. In their article on some birds they had observed in that island, S. Roch and Edward Newton said it was "tolerably common" in 1861, but they say little else about it, perhaps because it was so common. The specimen illustrated so sensitively by Wolf, presumably based on a skin collected by them, has a heavily barred belly suggesting that it was a youngster.

The Madagascar Buzzard has powerful feet for a bird of its size. It uses them to good effect when capturing its prey, which consists of a variety of animals, such as frogs, reptiles, smaller ground mammals and insects, especially locusts. Madagascar's only buzzard occurs in all woodland and savannah environments and open country, where it occurs from sea level up to six thousand feet or more. It is commonly seen soaring, but is also a familiar sight perched on trees, posts, anthills and rocks – anywhere providing a commanding view of the surrounding countryside.

J.Wolf del et lith.   M.&N.Hanhart,Imp.^t

BUTEO BRACHYPTERUS.

Northern Rough-legged Hawk (1864)

ROUGH-LEGGED BUZZARD, *Archibuteo lagopus*, (now Northern Rough-legged Hawk, *Buteo lagopus*). Hand-coloured lithograph by H.C. Richter from an original drawing by J. Wolf, pl. 7 (in Part 6, 1864) from Vol. 1 of J. Gould's *The Birds of Great Britain*, 1862–73. Size of plate 21¾" × 14½".

Gould obtained the bird illustrated here from Horace William Wheelwright, a gentleman who had spent some years in Sweden, where he would have had ample opportunity to study the Northern Rough-legged Hawk (which he would have known as the Rough-legged Buzzard). Wheelwright had particularly noticed the abundance of this species in the Quickiock district of Lapland, where lemmings, its main prey, abounded. Wolf would also have seen it often on the European mainland. Gould does not say whether his illustrated specimen originated from Sweden or from Britain. Neither could he decide if it was present in the New World as well as the Old, although ornithologists now agree that it has a circumpolar distribution.

The Northern Rough-legged Hawk, which reaches Britain across the North Sea, appears to have been plentiful there occasionally during the early years of the nineteenth century, but perhaps no more than twenty were being reported annually during the later years of the twentieth. Its plumage has a dark and a light phase but, in either phase, individuals from North America do not differ significantly from their Scandinavian and Russian counterparts. The plumage of the young bird virtually resembles that of its parents.

ARCHIBUTEO LAGOPUS.

J. Wolf and H.C.Richter, del et lith.

Walter & Cohn, Imp.

Blyth's Hawk-eagle (1863)

BLYTH'S HAWK-EAGLE, *Spizaetus alboniger*. Hand-coloured lithograph by H.C. Richter from an original drawing by J. Wolf, pl. 10 (in Part 15, 1863) from Vol. 1 of J. Gould's *The Birds of Asia*, 1849–83. Size of plate 21½″ × 14½″.

The Hawk-eagles of the genus *Spizaetus* occur mostly within the tropics around the globe, the species shown here being found in mountain forests in Thailand, Burma, the Malay peninsula and Borneo. Each of the few species has a crest or similar head ornament, a strong and deeply hooked beak and powerful talons. These features are well seen in Wolf's striking picture of Blyth's Hawk-eagle. Wolf chose to portray the bird from a low viewpoint and this makes it appear much larger than it is. With a maximum body length of about twenty-one inches, it is one of the smaller Hawk-eagles. The largest, a bird about ten inches longer, was trained for falconry by Japanese falconers.

Blyth's Hawk-eagle will sit for hours, often with its crest erect, but can fly energetically, even through the foliage of trees, and soar gracefully. Its usual prey consists of small arboreal mammals, bats and birds, but occasionally it takes domestic poultry. Its most unattractive feature, perhaps, is its cry – a shrill scream. Wolf's picture invests it with a kind of nobility which it may not deserve.

SPIZAËTUS ALBONIGER, *Blyth.*

J. Wolf and H.C.Richter, del. et lith.

Walter & Cohn, Imp.

Wallace's Hawk-eagle (1868)

WALLACE'S HAWK-EAGLE, *Spizaetus nanus*. Hand-coloured lithograph by J. Wolf, pl. 1 from *Ibis* (New Series), Vol. 4, 1868, illustrating an article by A.R. Wallace, "On the raptorial birds of the Malay Archipelago". Size of plate 8½″ × 5″.

Alfred Russel Wallace spent fifteen months in Borneo in the mid-1850s and made a considerable addition to our knowledge of its natural history, making a large collection of animal specimens and paying particular attention to the orang-utan, the island's most celebrated mammal. Unfortunately, he was unable to collect many birds. He explains why in *The Malay Archipelago*, that most fascinating of travel books. "During my stay in Borneo", he says, "I had no hunter to shoot for me regularly, and, being myself fully occupied with insects, I did not succeed in obtaining a very good collection of the birds or Mammalia, many of which, however, are well known." His collection included a single example of the bird illustrated here. It proved to be new to science and he christened it *Spizaetus nanus*. Fittingly it is now known as Wallace's Hawk-eagle.

This nineteen-inch-long bird – easily recognized by its crest, its cinnamon underparts streaked and barred with black and its tail with three dark bands – occurs in Java and Sumatra as well as Borneo. As he did with the subject of the following plate, Wolf successfully reconstructed the probable appearance of a living bird from the dried skin of a unique specimen which would probably have shown gunshot damage.

$\frac{1}{3}$

J Wolf. lith.

M & N Hanhart imp

SPIZAETUS NANUS.

Ayres's Eagle (1862)

AYRES'S HAWK-EAGLE, *Spizaetus ayresii* (now Ayres's Eagle, *Hieraetus ayresii*).
Hand-coloured lithograph by J. Jury from an original drawing by J. Wolf,
pl. 4 from *Ibis*, Vol. 4, 1862, illustrating an article by J.H. Gurney, "A fourth
additional list of birds received from Natal". Size of plate 8½″ × 5″.

Joseph Wolf designed the first known portraits of several bird species, for
he was often commissioned to illustrate articles describing species supposedly new to science. The lithograph reproduced here, for example,
accompanied an article by John Henry Gurney, who had received some birds
collected in Natal by Thomas Ayres. Gurney's description of the bird – he
received only one specimen from Ayres – is pitifully brief: "*Male*. Iris light
yellow; base of bill ash-colour, tip black; cere and feet greenish yellow."
Inexplicably, he thought it unnecessary to describe the rest of the bird or to
give its measurements (it attains a length of nineteen inches). Without Wolf's
picture no one could have recognized it again.

   The additional information supplied by Gurney was minimal: "This bird
was shot near the coast in a very dense bush; it is extremely rare here. I know
nothing of its habits; the stomach was perfectly empty." It is not as rare as
Gurney thought but it is uncommon over most of its range, which
encompasses much of Africa south of the Sahara. The egg-stealing habits of
certain monkeys probably contribute to its scarcity.

Wolf et J Jury lith.

M. & N Hanhart Imp

SPIZAETUS AYRESII.

Golden Eagle (1863)

GOLDEN EAGLE, *Aquila chrysaetos*. Hand-coloured lithograph by H.C. Richter from an original drawing by J. Wolf, pl. 2 (in Part 3, 1863) from Vol. 1 of J. Gould's *The Birds of Great Britain*, 1862–73. Size of plate 21¾" × 14½".

Gould was anxious about the future of the Golden Eagle. "As civilization advances," he says, "this noble bird, the lord of our ancient forests, will either become extirpated or driven to seek an asylum in parts of the country where nature still preserves a savage aspect. High cultivation and its presence are incompatible; the lamb and the Eagle can never dwell together in peace . . . and the time is probably not far distant when it will no longer have a place in the avifauna of the British Islands." He produces some statistics to justify his anxiety. "To show the amount of destruction dealt out to this noble bird and the Sea Eagle, the Sutherlandshire Expedition of Naturalists state that the number of Eagles paid for between March 1831 and March 1834 was 171, besides 53 nestlings or eggs; and a gamekeeper in the south-west of that county trapped 15 Eagles in three months of 1847, and almost as many in the winter of 1850–51." Towards the end of the twentieth century Scotland was almost its only remaining British stronghold; but its numbers there seemed to have increased, so the future of the Golden Eagle in Britain may not be so bleak as Gould feared.

The soaring flight of the Golden Eagle is a joy to behold. "It may often be seen in fine weather," says Gould, "sailing to a vast height towards the blue vault of heaven, apparently for no other purpose than that of pleasure; and its evolutions are graceful and majestic while thus engaged." He says that the eyrie shown in the background of this picture was drawn by Wolf. According to Palmer, "Wolf was able to pay a spring visit to Black Mount, on the estate of a nobleman near Glencoe. Here, under the guidance of an old keeper, he could watch a couple of eyries day after day." That must have been an exciting and valuable experience for the artist.

AQUILA CHRYSAËTOS, *Briss*

Spotted Eagle (1870)

Spotted Eagle, *Aquila naevia* (now *Aquila clanga*). Hand-coloured lithograph by H.C. Richter from an original drawing by J. Wolf, pl. 3 (in Part 17, 1870) from Vol. 1 of J. Gould's *The Birds of Great Britain*, 1862–73. Size of plate 21¾″ × 14½″.

Gould knew of two specimens of what was presumably the Spotted Eagle which had been killed in England and of two others shot in Ireland, evidence too slender for this species to have a permanent place on the British list but sufficient for him to describe and illustrate it in his *Birds of Great Britain*. Easily confused with the slightly smaller Lesser Spotted Eagle, it is resident in lowland forests near water, from eastern Europe across to China. It preys on small mammals but will also come to carrion.

Edward Hearle Rodd published an account of the first "English" example of this bird, killed at Hawk's Wood in Cornwall on 4 December 1860. "The bird was first observed in a tree," he says, "from which, on the approach of the shooting party, instead of soaring, it shuffled down, and scrambled under some rocks; its condition was beyond the average of birds of prey, large masses of fat encircling the gizzard, which, on dissection, was entirely empty; one of the wing-bones was broken, but whether with shot or otherwise I could not determine; the body, wings, and every part of the bird exhibited the most perfect form; but probably the injury above mentioned prevented it from taking flight. It was a male in the first year's plumage, and weighed 4 lbs. 1 oz." Gould says the bird in the foreground of this picture was a youngster, that in the background an adult. He does not say they are "English" specimens.

AQUILA NÆVIA.

J.Wolf & H.C.Richter, del et lith.

Walter, Imp.

Tawny Eagle (1865)

TAWNY EAGLE, *Aquila naevioides* (now *Aquila rapax*). Hand-coloured lithograph by J. Wolf, pl. 5 from *Ibis* (New Series), Vol. 1, 1865, illustrating an article by Lord Lilford, "Notes on the ornithology of Spain". Size of plate 8½″ × 5″.

Thomas Lyttleton Powys, Fourth Baron of Lilford, was an outstanding ornithologist, although for a long time he was unable to walk but compelled to observe birds from a Bath chair. Towards the end of his life he published his *Coloured Figures of the Birds of the British Islands*, an authoritative book in seven volumes, but this plate comes from an article about the birds of Spain he published in 1865. In the article he comments briefly on the Tawny Eagle. "I have, at the present time," he says, "three of this species alive in my possession, from two of which Mr. Wolf took the sketches for the Plate. The darker bird I have had for nearly three years, and he or she (for I am ignorant of the sex) has altered very little in appearance during the time, though the dark markings have, I think, somewhat increased in breadth and number. The light specimen, which I obtained last year, I consider to be an immature bird, and, from its small size, it is, I think, a male."

The Tawny Eagle breeds in Africa, south-eastern Europe eastwards to Mongolia, and from Iran to Burma. Specialists recognize several races which vary greatly in colour, from nearly white to almost black. A medium-sized eagle of treeless or bushy plains and deserts, it usually flies low and preys upon small animals.

J.Wolf.del.et.lith.

M.& N Hanhart imp

AQUILA NAEVIOIDES.

Wahlberg's Eagle (1862)

AQUILA DESMURSII (now Wahlberg's Eagle, *Aquila wahlbergi*). Hand-coloured lithograph by J. Wolf, pl. 77, 1862 from *Transactions of the Zoological Society of London*, Vol. 4, 1851–62, illustrating an article by J.H. Gurney, "Remarks on *Aquila desmursii*". Size of plate 12″ × 9″.

Wahlberg's Eagle is a resident of the savannah areas of Africa south of the Sahara and migrates locally. Its plumage varies considerably, some individuals being dark brown, some very pale and others of an intermediate hue. In his account of this small eagle John Henry Gurney says, "both adult and immature birds appear liable to have their plumage exceedingly bleached by the action of the tropical sun." Three contrasting states of plumage are shown in this plate, which portrays specimens that Wolf was able to study in the collection of the Norwich Museum.

An unobtrusive and rather silent bird, Wahlberg's Eagle prefers cultivated areas or other places not far from human habitation. It is often seen perched upon trees or soaring above them at heights between three hundred and four hundred feet. Moving through the bush in a series of short flights from tree to tree, it pounces on small animals such as mice, although in the non-breeding season it tends to drift northwards to take advantage of the hunting afforded by grass and brush fires. Sometimes it will attack other birds, or even small gazelles. Courageous or foolhardy, this is remarkable behaviour for a bird with a maximum body length of twenty-five inches.

White-tailed Eagle (1863)

SEA EAGLE, *Haliaetus albicilla* (now White-tailed Eagle). Hand-coloured lithograph by H.C. Richter from an original drawing by J. Wolf, pl. 4 (in Part 3, 1863) from Vol. 1 of J. Gould's *The Birds of Great Britain*, 1862–73. Size of plate 21¾″ × 14½″.

This bird used to be common in Europe and Russia but disappeared from most of Europe during the nineteenth and twentieth centuries. It still breeds in parts of southern Russia and along the southern coasts of Greenland, where it attains its largest size. As the airborne bird in this picture shows, the huge wings of the White-tailed Eagle dwarf its head and tail. The heavy yellowish bill displayed by the female in the foreground is another characteristic feature of this massive bird. Unlike the Golden Eagle, its flight is laboured and clumsy, soaring with flattened wings and projecting head. It is not fussy about how or where it obtains its food, being equally content with fish taken from the surface of the water, with sea birds or various mammals, or even with carrion.

It was common in Britain long ago but was systematically destroyed so that, except in some remote sites in the Shetlands and Orkneys, it had ceased to breed there by the end of the nineteenth century. It would sometimes make an eyrie on an island in a Scottish loch, assuming that the site would be safe from the destructive influence of human beings, but sometimes it failed to estimate the depth of the surrounding water correctly and its enemy waded across and stole the contained eggs. Sometimes swimming was considered necessary to achieve this purpose, but this could be a dangerous procedure because the bird would beat its enemy down into the water with its wings. Fortunately there is a chance that the White-tailed Eagle will soon be re-established as a breeding bird in Scotland.

J Wolf and M.C Richter del et lith.

Walter & Cohn, Imp.

HALIAËTUS ALBICILLA.

Steller's Sea-eagle (1844)

L'AIGLE DE MER GÉANT, *Halietos pelagicus* (now Steller's Sea-eagle, *Haliaetus pelagicus*). Hand-coloured lithograph by J. Wolf, pl. 4 (1844) from P.F. von Siebold's *Fauna Japonica. Description des Oiseaux*, 1844–50. Size of plate 15½″ × 11″.

An imposing bird, up to forty inches in body length and with a wing span to match, Steller's Sea-eagle – named after Georg Wilhelm Steller, one of the earliest investigators of Pacific natural history – lives along the coasts of north-eastern Asia southwards as far as Korea. It winters in Japan, which is how it came to be included in Siebold's *Fauna Japonica*. Much larger than the related Bald Eagle of North America and the White-tailed Eagle (illustrated on the previous plate), its large, bright-yellow beak is more powerful than that of any other bird of prey. The plumage of the adults is also very striking, the predominant black colour being offset by brilliant white on the wings, thighs and tail, features not well seen in this picture because the bird Wolf used as his model was a female still in the dress of immaturity. A dark phase of this bird – all black except for the characteristic pale grey streaks on the head and white tail and tail coverts – occurs in Korea.

Contrasting with its imposing appearance are its eating habits. It will prey upon large or medium-sized birds but is happy to feed on dead or dying fish after they have spawned or, in their absence, will scavenge offal from slaughterhouses. In keeping with its great size, Steller's Sea-eagle builds a huge nest, up to eight feet across, in which it usually rears just one youngster. A giant among giants, this bird is impressive in everything but its attitude to food.

$\frac{1}{3}$.

Egyptian Vulture (1872)

EGYPTIAN VULTURE, *Neophron percnopterus*. Hand-coloured lithograph by H.C. Richter from an original drawing by J. Wolf, pl. 1 (in Part 21, 1872) from Vol. 1 of J. Gould's *The Birds of Great Britain*, 1862–73. Size of plate 21¾″ × 14½″.

This picture portrays the smallest and most abundant of the four European species of vulture, distinguished from all other birds of prey by its small, pointed head and long, thin bill. From Gould's comments it seems that the first Egyptian Vulture to be recorded in Britain had been shot in Somersetshire in October 1825, the second in Essex in September 1868. The first was discovered "feeding upon the carcass of a dead sheep, and had so gorged itself with the carrion as to be unable or unwilling to fly to any great distance at a time, and was therefore approached and shot without much difficulty". It was described as a young bird of the first or second year. The Essex bird, when surprised by a labourer, was feeding upon the blood of a goose it had killed. "The bird flew away," says Gould, "and the man loaded his gun. Presently it came again and hovered over the spot in hopes of another spell at the blood; but his fate was sealed, and he fell dead to the labourer's shot." Gould, who examined the bird later, says, "it was from this specimen that the reduced figure in my Plate was taken." He is presumably referring to the smaller of the two figures.

The Egyptian Vulture, which is native to most of Africa, southern Europe, the Middle East and India, must have seemed a very exotic visitor when it appeared in two English parishes, for, as Gould points out, "the British Islands are not a favourite place of resort for any of the Vultures."

J Wolf & HC Richter del et lith.

NEOPHRON PERCNOPTERUS.

Walter Imp.

Indian Black Vulture (1860)

BLACK VULTURE, *Otogyps calvus* (now Indian Black Vulture, *Sarcogyps calvus*). Hand-coloured lithograph by H.C. Richter from an original drawing by J. Wolf, pl. 1 (in Part 12, 1860) from Vol. 1 of J. Gould's *The Birds of Asia*, 1849–83. Size of plate 21½″ × 14½″.

This is the first plate in the first volume of *Birds of Asia*, a book Gould did not see finished in his lifetime. While the book was in progress he would often call at Wolf's studio, help himself to one of the artist's cigars, produce a bird's skin and ask for an immediate water-colour sketch of it. Wolf did not like this kind of cajolery, although he often complied. He provided original drawings for eight birds of prey in the first volume of *The Birds of Asia* and, when Gould was old and infirm, provided drawings of other birds to help illustrate the seventh volume.

The Indian Black Vulture (also known as the Pondicherry Vulture) is a conspicuous feature of India, being present everywhere in that very large peninsula. Its range also includes Burma and the Malay peninsula. Although timid and retiring, it will sometimes kill for food, its powerful beak enabling it to rip open fresh carcasses of even the larger mammals. Unlike most other vultures, it is not gregarious and does not squabble over carrion with other birds. The nest, a large platform of sticks lined with straw and leaves, may be constructed in a tall tree or a low bush, and in it the bird lays one pure-white egg. (In this lithograph, incidentally, the skin of the head has been painted too dark; it should be yellowish red.)

OTOGYPS CALVUS.

J. Wolf and H.C.Richter, del. et lith.

Hullmandel & Walton, Imp.

Griffon Vulture (1880)

GRIFFON VULTURE, *Gyps fulvus*. Hand-coloured lithograph by W. Hart from an original drawing by J. Wolf, pl. 319 (in Parts 77–9, 1880) from Vol. 5 of H. E. Dresser's *A History of the Birds of Europe*, 1871–96. Size of plate 12" × 9½".

When working on his nine-volume *History of the Birds of Europe*, Henry Eeles Dresser commissioned Wolf to make drawings of the birds of prey. Dresser had a high opinion of Wolf's work. "Where he excels and surpasses any animal painter I know of", he says, in a letter to A.H. Palmer, "is that not only is he an excellent *artist*, but he so thoroughly understands the pose and characteristic points of the animals he paints, whether animals or birds. There are certain characteristic peculiarities in every species which can only be distinguished by anyone who has made a life study of them; and these Wolf has an inborn power of transmitting to his canvas." This fine study of the Griffon Vulture, although several steps removed from Wolf's original conception, reveals something of that inborn power.

Common in mountainous districts from southern Europe to northern India (South Africa has its own distinctly paler race), the Griffon Vulture soars for long periods searching for carcasses of large mammals. Once a carcass is found, there is a pecking order among the assembled birds of this species which determines that the more dominant of them eat first. The whitish collar or ruff is characteristic but is seldom visible.

J.Wolf del.

W.Hart lith.

GRIFFON VULTURE.

GYPS FULVUS.

Hen Harrier (1879)

HEN HARRIER, *Circus cyaneus*. Hand-coloured lithograph by W. Hart from an original drawing by J. Wolf, pl. 329 (in Parts 75–6, 1879) from Vol. 5 of H.E. Dresser's *A History of the Birds of Europe*, 1871–96. Size of plate 12″ × 9½″.

In this picture a male Hen Harrier perches on a branch while a female hovers in the distance. The picture shows the great contrast between the plumage of the two sexes and gives a good idea of the way a solitary bird hovers low over a favourable hunting-ground, quartering it thoroughly in search of insects, reptiles, small mammals and birds. Because of its thoroughness, it has always been disliked by gamekeepers of grouse moors, among others, and they almost annihilated it from Britain during the second half of the nineteenth century. Towards the end of the twentieth century, however, it had recovered from this persecution sufficiently to become Britain's commonest nesting harrier. Occasionally it will chase other birds, even over water, and will take dead fish which have been washed up on shore or which are floating on the surface of the water. A correspondent of Dresser's, having shot a Hen Harrier, found a half-devoured partridge at the spot whence it had taken flight. "This had been killed, as appeared by the feathers, at a short distance, but carried to the edge of a splash of water, where the plunderer had an opportunity of washing his beak and claws between every mouthful."

The Hen Harrier occurs over most of the temperate zone of the northern hemisphere. In North America, where it is known as the Marsh Hawk, it generally resembles the European bird but the differences are sufficient for it to be considered a separate subspecies.

329

J.Wolf del

W.Hart.Lith.

½

HENHARRIER.

CIRCUS CYANEUS.

Montagu's Harrier (1878)

MONTAGU'S HARRIER, *Circus cineraceus* (now *Circus pygargus*). Hand-coloured lithograph by E. Neale from an original drawing by J. Wolf, pl. 328 (in Parts 67–8, 1878) from Vol. 5 of H.E. Dresser's *A History of the Birds of Europe*, 1871–96. Size of plate 12″ × 9½″.

A bird of Europe and central Asia which winters as far away as Africa and India, Montagu's Harrier is named after George Montagu, who revolutionized the study of birds in Britain with his *Ornithological Dictionary*, published in 1802. Montagu was also the first to clarify the identifying characters of this bird. Although easily confused with the Hen Harrier (the subject of the previous plate) and the Pallid Harrier (the subject of the following plate) the essential diagnostic feature of the male is well displayed by the bird in the foreground of this lithograph: the narrow black band on the raised wing coverts. The figure of the female on the left, though well drawn, could pass for the female of either of the other two species as well, the features which separate all three requiring an expert eye to be distinguished.

This small but elegant harrier frequents open grassland, swamps, lowland heaths, scrub, reed beds, forest plantations and other cultivated land. It soars or hovers, flies low over the ground and drops on to its prey, which includes mice and other small mammals, reptiles, birds and their eggs, grasshoppers and other large insects. When involved in pairing displays, it dives with wings and tail spread out, producing loud drumming noises as it does so.

J.Wolf del. E.Neale lith.

$\frac{1}{2}$

Hanhart imp

MONTAGU'S HARRIER.
CIRCUS CINERACEUS.

Pallid Harrier (1878)

PALLID HARRIER, *Circus swainsoni* (now *Circus macrourus*). Hand-coloured lithograph by E. Neale from an original drawing by J. Wolf, pl. 330 (in Parts 67–8, 1878) from Vol. 5 of H.E. Dresser's *A History of the Birds of Europe*, 1871–96. Size of plate 12″ × 9½″.

When commenting upon Joseph Wolf's published illustrations, A. H. Palmer is very complimentary about those he contributed to Dresser's *History of the Birds of Europe*. Describing this work as "one of the most fascinating, comfortable, and useful books a lover of birds can covet", he says that we can all appreciate the interest of the descriptions and the vivacity and truthfulness of attitude in the fifteen designs which Wolf did for his old and intimate friend. The chief of these are now to be found in the family *Falconidae*; and the designs were boldly sketched on a large scale in Wolf's favourite 'charcoal grey'."

Palmer reproduces two of these designs, one of them being the original drawing for this excellent illustration of the Pallid Harrier, a study of the adult male (right) and female of a bird difficult for ornithologists to distinguish from the Hen Harrier and Montagu's Harrier, the subjects of the two previous plates. It must have been hard for Wolf to capture the differences between these birds in his charcoal-grey designs, and almost impossible for those who made and coloured the lithographs from them.

$\frac{1}{2}$

J.Wolf del E.Neale lith.

Hanhart imp

PALLID HARRIER.
CIRCUS SWAINSONI.

Marsh Harrier (1878)

MARSH HARRIER, *Circus aeruginosus*. Hand-coloured lithograph by J. Smit from an original drawing by J. Wolf, pl. 326 (in Parts 71–2, 1878) from Vol. 5 of H.E. Dresser's *A History of the Birds of Europe*, 1871–96. Size of plate 12″ × 9½″.

The Marsh Harrier ranges from Europe across Russia to Siberia and Japan, occurs in Australasia and Indonesia in the Pacific, and has toeholds on the islands of Madagascar and Reunion in the Indian Ocean. In keeping with such a large and scattered distribution, this buzzard-like harrier assumes different guises according to location, specialists distinguishing several races or subspecies mostly by plumage differences. Shown here is the typical form, represented by an adult female (left) and an immature male.

When discussing the Marsh Harrier in his account of the birds of Northumberland and Durham, John Hancock (quoted by Dresser), refers to a nauseating example of its persecution in the first quarter of the nineteenth century. "In 1823 I took a nest of it, with four eggs, on the moors of Wemmergill, near Middleton-in-Teesdale, the shooting-box of the late Lord Strathmore. Both parent birds had been shot or trapped by the gamekeeper, and formed part of his museum, nailed against the stable walls. This collection was made up of Hawks, Owls, Daws, Buzzards, and such like 'vermin', both biped and quadruped, being altogether one of the largest and most disgusting I have ever seen. It is now quite impossible in the north of England for any gamekeeper to form such another museum to bear witness to his zeal and ignorance, as the so-called vermin no longer exist." The Marsh Harrier was extinct in Britain by the end of the nineteenth century, but it staged a comeback during the twentieth. Towards the close of the twentieth century its continued survival there into the twenty-first seemed assured.

J.Wolf del. J.Smit lith.

Hanhart imp.

MARSH HARRIER.

1. YOUNG MALE.
2. ADULT FEMALE.

Marsh Harrier (1863)

Circus Spilonotus (now Marsh Harrier, *Circus aeruginosus spilonotus*). Hand-coloured lithograph by J. Wolf, pl. 5 from *Ibis*, Vol. 5, 1863, illustrating an article by R. Swinhoe, "The ornithology of Formosa, or Taiwan". Size of plate 8½" × 5".

The study of natural history filled the spare time of Robert Swinhoe, a British consular official, during his tour of duty in Taiwan. In 1863 his pioneering studies of the birds of that island were published in a long article in *Ibis*. "In this, my favourite class," he says, "I spared no pains or expense to make as large a collection and gain as much information as possible. I employed a vast number of native hunters and stuffers, and collected very large series of every available species and their eggs."

He says further, "I have been blamed by some naturalists for allowing Mr. Gould to reap the fruits of my labours, in having the privilege of describing most of my novelties, I must briefly state, in explanation, that I returned to England elate with the fine new species I had discovered, and was particularly anxious that they should comprise one entire part of Mr. Gould's fine work on the Birds of Asia, still in progress. On an interview with Mr. Gould, I found that the only way to achieve this was to consent to his describing the entire series to be figured, as he would include none in the part but novelties which he should himself name and describe. I somewhat reluctantly complied, but as he has done me the honour to name the most important species after me, I suppose I have no right to complain." Poor Swinhoe; like Wolf, he learnt the hard way that John Gould was not the most generous of men.

As Swinhoe and his "vast number of native hunters" had obtained no specimens of this race of the Marsh Harrier, he had supplied Wolf with a male and female from Amoy, a small island off the Chinese coast near Taiwan. This race has a wide distribution over eastern Asia and winters in some Indonesian islands, Taiwan, Japan and elsewhere. The juveniles and adult females are darker than the typical form of the Marsh Harrier, but the males are strikingly different, as may be seen by comparing this plate with the previous one.

J. Wolf, del. et lith,

M. & N. Hanhart, Imp

CIRCUS SPILONOTUS.

Southern Banded Snake-eagle (1862)

SOUTHERN BANDED SNAKE-EAGLE, *Circaetus fasciolatus*. Hand-coloured litho-graph by J. Jennens from an original drawing by J. Wolf, pl. 3 from *Ibis*, Vol. 3, 1862, illustrating an article by J.H. Gurney, "An additional list of birds received from Natal". Size of plate 8½″ × 5″.

Thomas Ayres of Natal sent many bird specimens with ornithological notes to John Henry Gurney in England. The Southern Banded Snake-eagle was one of the more interesting of these. "This is a very rare bird, frequenting the dense bush along the coast," says Ayres. The coast in question extends from Tanganyika to Natal and encompasses the entire range of this bird. Ayres sent a specimen to Gurney, but the one illustrated by Wolf came from the fine bird collection housed in the Norwich Museum, the source of several birds the artist used as models.

A medium-sized eagle, clumsy in flight, the Southern Banded Snake-eagle has four transverse bands on the tail and, like other members of its genus, it has scaly legs which, experts think, help to deflect snakebites. It occurs chiefly in forested country and river valleys or near swampy ground, but also frequents open savannah country occasionally. From its usual perch on a tree it swoops down on its prey, mostly snakes and lizards. Even now little is known abouts its habits.

Ibis 1862 Pl.3

J.Wolf.del.
J.Jennens,lith.

M.& N.Hanhart,Imp.

CIRCAETUS FASCIOLATUS.

Sulawesi Serpent-eagle (1860)

RUFOUS-BREASTED SPILORNIS, *Spilornis rufipectus* (now Sulawesi Serpent-eagle). Hand-coloured lithograph by H.C. Richter from an original drawing by J. Wolf, pl. 9 (in Part 12, 1860) from Vol. 1 of J. Gould's *The Birds of Asia*, 1849–83. Size of plate 21½" × 14".

Gould says that the specimen illustrated in this plate "was sent by Mr. Wallace from Celebes, and was obtained by him in the vicinity of Macassar". The sender was Alfred Russel Wallace whose travels in Indonesia resulted in the discovery of many animals of all kinds. He would have collected this nineteen-inch-long bird near Macassar, the capital of Celebes (now Sulawesi), during the dry season of 1856 or 1857, when he made several excursions in search of birds, mammals, insects and snails. In his delightful book, *The Malay Archipelago*, Wallace has a lot to say about the remarkable animals he found in this tropical island, but he is silent about this bird.

A very dark-coloured bird which shows strikingly barred wings in flight, it lives in grassy savannah country, less often in forests, and prefers higher ground. Like some other birds of prey, it is attracted to grass fires because they make it easier to spot the lizards, snakes, and small mammals which constitute its prey. As Celebes is now known as Sulawesi it makes sense to call this little-known bird the Sulawesi Serpent-eagle. Fortunately, its scientific name, having no political connotation, remains unchanged.

SPILORNIS RUFIPECTUS, *Gould*

J. Gould and H.C.Richter del. & lith.   Hullmandel & Walton, Imp.

Osprey (1870)

OSPREY, *Pandion haliaetus*. Hand-coloured lithograph by H.C. Richter from an original drawing by J. Wolf, pl. 5 (in Part 17, 1870) from Vol. 1 of J. Gould's *The Birds of Great Britain*, 1862–73. Size of plate 21¾″ × 14½″.

This strikingly marked bird has spread itself around the world very successfully. It breeds throughout most of the northern hemisphere and migrates to lands in the south-west Pacific, Arabia, Africa and South America. Conspicuous because of its distinctive plumage and its dramatic fishing habits, familiar because of its frequent appearances on television, the Osprey (sometimes called the Fish Hawk) is one of the most publicized birds in the world. Everyone knows how it dives into the water and rises with a fish grasped firmly in its talons. Everyone knows it is a bird threatened on all sides by its main enemies – us. Everyone – if only at a distance – loves the Osprey, just as everyone loves the panda.

In several ways, not all obvious, it is unique. Anatomically it is related on the one hand to the true falcons, on the other to the eagles and Old World vultures, but it also has features separating it from such birds. It feeds only on fish and builds a colossal nest. It is unremarkable close up when doing nothing, magnificent at a distance when hunting. The opening sentence of Gould's description of this bird was still relevant well over a century after he wrote it. "Notwithstanding the persecution to which this interesting bird has been subjected, especially of late years, a persecution so unrelenting that it has almost amounted to its extirpation from the British Islands, the Osprey still forms a part of their avifauna, especially of that portion of them denominated Scotland, and will ever remain associated with the fine lochs and deserted castles of that country." To emphasize that association, Gould says that the fish held by the bird in the foreground of Wolf's picture is a Scottish trout.

PANDION HALIAËTUS.

J. Wolf & H.C.Richter, del. et lith. Walter, Imp.

Gyrfalcon ("Norwegian Falcon") (1872)

NORWEGIAN FALCON or GYRFALCON, *Falco gyrfalco* (now Gyrfalcon, *Falco rusticolus*). Hand-coloured lithograph by H.C. Richter from an original drawing by J. Wolf, pl. 16 (in Part 22, 1872) from Vol. 1 of J. Gould's *The Birds of Great Britain*, 1862–73. Size of plate 21¾″ × 14½″.

This is the last of six illustrations of the Gyrfalcon in *Birds of Great Britain*. Gould supplied a few prefatory remarks to explain why he had included in his book the bird he called the Norwegian Falcon. "Without a few words of explanation," he says, "it might appear to some of my readers that I am extending the present work beyond its proper limits by figuring on the opposite plate a bird which has never yet been identified as a visitor to the British Islands; but such is not my wish. It is given because the chances are that, although not recognized, the bird does occasionally visit us, and that I may be enabled to throw a clearer light upon a subject of great importance than I could do by leaving it undelineated. To render my meaning more apparent, I must inform those of my readers who are not well versed in ornithology that it is a question among naturalists whether the Norwegian, the Iceland, and the Greenland Falcons are one and the same species, or whether each possesses characters of sufficient importance to distinguish it from its congeners. Whatever conclusions some may have arrived at with regard to their specific value, I for my own part cannot but regard them as distinct from each other." He goes on to say, "The true Gyrfalcon or Norwegian bird is by far the darkest in colour, and somewhat the smallest in size."

Ever since Gould's day experts have disagreed about the relationships of the so-called Norwegian, Iceland and Greenland Falcons, but it is now widely accepted that they merely represent forms (or phases) of one species, the Gyrfalcon, distinguished from each other mostly by differences in their plumage. The Gyrfalcon has a circumpolar distribution and is the largest falcon within its area. Gould says that this plate portrays an adult and a "young bird of the first autumn".

FALCO GYRFALCO, *Linn.*

Norwegian Falcon, adult and young.

Gyrfalcon ("Iceland Falcon") (c. 1844)

L<small>E</small> T<small>IERCELET</small> H<small>AGARD</small> <small>DE</small> F<small>AUCON</small> D'I<small>SLANDE</small> (Gyrfalcon, *Falco rusticolus*). Hand-coloured lithograph by J. Wolf, with additional details by C. Scheuren, pl. 2 (c. 1844) from H. Schlegel and A.H. Verster van Wulverhorst's *Traité de Fauconnerie*, 1844–53. Size of plate 26½″ × 19½″.

The Gyrfalcon, especially the "Iceland" form, is given special and lengthy treatment in Schlegel and Wulverhorst's magnificent treatise on falconry. The authors commissioned Wolf to make several portraits of it and this may be the best of them. It shows a male specimen of what they called the Iceland Falcon reproduced life-size. Its upper and under surfaces are lighter in colour than those of the so-called "Norwegian" bird, illustrated on the previous plate, with the tail bars perfectly defined. It is the form of the Gyrfalcon prevalent in Iceland.

When falconry was virtually the sport of kings Iceland was the source of the most highly regarded birds. The King of Denmark sent a vessel there annually to bring away as many of them as could be caught. These were intended either for his own falconers or, as presents, for the use of other royal or princely households in Europe and the Orient. The "Icelander" was superior in flight to the "ordinary" Gyrfalcon but was of a more tractable and gentle disposition. It would pounce on its prey with more lofty stoops, the female being used to catch the hare, the male to catch the heron, the kite and the Common Buzzard. A male Icelander was once seen to strike the head from the neck of a heron by a single blow in the air. Judging from the numbers shipped to Denmark, the Icelander was once abundant in Iceland. Alas, it is abundant there no longer.

Dessiné par M.WOLF, accessoires par C.SCHL....   Publié chez A. ARNZ et Comp. à LEIDE.

LE TIERCELET HAGARD DE FAUCON D'ISLANDE.

Gyrfalcon ("Greenland Falcon, Dark Race") (1872)

GREENLAND FALCON, DARK RACE, *Falco candicans* (now Gyrfalcon, *Falco rusticolus*). Hand–coloured lithograph by W. Hart from an original drawing by J. Wolf, pl. 14 (in Part 22, 1873) from Vol. 1 of J. Gould's *The Birds of Great Britain*, 1862–73. Size of plate 21¾″ × 14½″.

Gould tried – unsuccessfully – to work out the relationship of the dark race of the so-called Greenland Falcon to the predominantly white race of this bird and the white race of the so-called Iceland Falcon. He had never seen two specimens of this dark race displaying the same markings, and this inconsistency puzzled him. "By some persons", he says, "it may be supposed that the individuals of the dark race change their plumage as they advance in age, and ultimately become white; but if the assertion of those ornithologists who have paid special attention to these Falcons, that the plumage they assume at their second moult is carried throughout life, be correct, this will not be the case; and that this theory is the true one would seem to be confirmed by the fact that a Greenland Falcon which lived for some years in the Gardens of the Zoological Society never exhibited any subsequent change." He concluded that the dark race was a mongrel produced by the interbreeding of the Greenland Falcon and the Iceland Falcon. We now know that plumage is an unreliable indicator of the origin and relationships of these birds.

"I cannot conclude", says Gould at the end of an unhelpful description of this bird, "without calling attention to the admirable delineations of all these large northern Falcons, for which I am indebted to the pencil of Mr. Wolf, whose abilities as an artist are so justly celebrated, and who thoroughly understands the subject. I trust they will be duly appreciated by the possessors of the present work."

FALCO CANDICANS.

Greenland Falcon, dark race, adult.

Gyrfalcon ("Greenland Falcon, Light Race") (1872)

GREENLAND FALCON, LIGHT RACE, *Falco candicans* (now Gyrfalcon, *Falco rusticolus*). Hand-coloured lithograph by H.C. Richter from an original drawing by J. Wolf, pl. 13 (in Part 22, 1872) from Vol. 1 of J. Gould's *The Birds of Great Britain*, 1862–73. Size of plate 21¾″ × 14½″.

This is probably Joseph Wolf's most powerful published study of a predatory bird. Often reproduced, it is at once dramatic and yet somehow tender without being sentimental. Gould thought a few words of explanation were necessary to enable the reader of his book to understand the picture. "The middle figure", he says, "represents an unusually light and beautiful young bird of the year, with tear-drop-like markings on the whole of the upper surface; the larger figure the adult, distinguished by having a small, somewhat heart-shaped spot at the tip of each feather of the upper surface, faint specks of brownish black on the under surface, and the tail creamy white." These are specimens of the white phase of the Gyrfalcon, formerly known as the Greenland Falcon. If they were "British" specimens they probably did come from Greenland, as do most Gyrfalcons which reach Britain, but this bird is predominantly white in the northern part of its range as a whole, not just in Greenland.

In the *Fauna Boreali Americana*, published in 1831, Sir John Richardson describes how a pair of Greenland Falcons had attacked him ten years earlier as he was climbing near their nest at Point Lake, away up in the North West Territories of Canada. "They flew in circles," he says, "uttering loud and harsh screams, and alternately stooping with such velocity that their motion through the air produced a loud rushing noise, they struck their claws within an inch or two of my head. I endeavoured, by keeping the barrel of my gun close to my cheek, and suddenly elevating its muzzle when they were in the act of striking, to ascertain whether they had the power of instantaneously changing the direction of their rapid course, and found that they invariably rose above the obstacle with the quickness of thought, showing equal acuteness of vision and power of motion."

13.

FALCO CANDICANS, *J.F. Gmel.*

Greenland Falcon, light race, adult and young.

J. Wolf & H.C. Richter, del. et lith.

Walter Imp.

Gyrfalcon ("Greenland Falcon – Hooded") (c. 1844)

LE GROENLANDAIS (Gyrfalcon, *Falco rusticolus*). Hand-coloured lithograph by J. Wolf, pl. 1 (c.1844) from H. Schlegel and H.A. Verster von Wulverhorst's *Traité de Fauconnerie*, 1844–53. Size of plate 26½″ × 19½″.

As Wolf had a profound and abiding interest in falconry, it is appropriate to complete his series of portraits of the Gyrfalcon with this compelling study of one wearing the trappings of the falconer's art. One of the dozen plates he prepared for the *Traité de Fauconnerie*, it shows a bird in the white phase, recently moulted, with jesses, bells and hood, perched on the falconer's fist. The jesses are two strips of leather attached to each leg and to a short leash. Together with the bells, which are made of silver or brass, the falconer uses them to control the bird. The decoratively feathered hood is removed when the falconer has accustomed the bird to its new situation. The original water-colour for this plate, once owned and treasured by John Gould, shows that these trappings were included in Wolf's original design. Someone else added most of the scenic details to the other plates Wolf contributed to the book.

In A.H. Palmer's biography of Wolf there are several references to the artist's knowledge of falcons and falconry. "It was once my good fortune", says Palmer, "to listen to a conversation between our friend and a keen Anglo-Indian falconer, which dealt with Sacres, Luggurs, and especially with the Shahins [Sakers, Laggers and Barbary Falcons], besides the notable career of certain of these birds. Wolf's real interest was evident; and it was also evident that he knew much of the respective merits of the different species, not only from an artistic, but from a sportsman's point of view."

Dessiné par M WOLF   Publié chez A ARNZ et Comp. à LEIDE

LE GROËNLANDAIS, FAUCON BLANC MUÉ.

Saker Falcon (1861)

SAKER FALCON, *Falco sacer* (now *Falco cherrug*). Hand-coloured lithograph by J. Smit from an original drawing by J. Wolf, pl. 33 from Vol. 1 of J. Wolf's *Zoological Sketches, First Series* (edited by D.W. Mitchell and P.L. Sclater), 1861. Size of plate 13½″ × 9½″.

The Saker Falcon, with a maximum length of twenty inches, is smaller than the Gyrfalcon but, like that bird, is a favourite with falconers. Found in the wild state in eastern Europe and western Asia, its hunting ability has been especially appreciated in the desert regions of North Africa. About the middle of the nineteenth century, an Arab sheikh told Henry Baker Tristram, an English traveller–naturalist, that one of these falcons had the same value as a thoroughbred horse and he was prepared to exchange the one for the other. The name Saker, incidentally, comes from *saqr*, the Arabic word for this bird.

The birds portrayed in Wolf's plate are described in the text of his *Zoological Sketches* (which was written by one of its two editors, each having been closely associated with the Gardens of the Zoological Society of London). "The accompanying plate represents the same individual of the species in two different stages. The upper figures were taken soon after the bird arrived in the Society's possession, and the lower, with the transverse bars on the shoulders, after it had attained fully adult plumage, having been for some time in the Gardens." So the picture gives the false impression that Wolf had three birds as models instead of one, but he was used to creating his compositions in this way. "From its extreme gentleness," the writer continues, "it came home in the most beautiful condition, on a very clever Arab block, specially adapted for travelling purposes. This is an inverted cone, the base covered with leather, and the apex prolonged by a pointed iron rod, of eighteen inches in length, by which it is easily fixed anywhere, on the floor of a room or in the open air upon the ground. The bird sits on the inverted base with great comfort, and without the possibility of injuring either tail or wings. The Saker moulted several times on this block, but at last, from want of exercise, became internally diseased, and we lost him."

Saker Falcon (1868)

SAKER FALCON, *Falco sacer* (now *Falco cherrug*). Hand-coloured lithograph by H.C. Richter from an original drawing by J. Wolf, pl. 5 (in Part 20, 1868) from Vol. 1 of J. Gould's *The Birds of Asia*, 1849–83. Size of plate 21½″ × 14½″.

A master of composition, J. Wolf never willingly introduced into a bird portrait any object which tended to draw attention away from the subject but he seems to have departed from that principle in this plate. The obvious difference between this and the previous plate is the addition here of a bright-green reptile clutched by the dominant bird's left claw. The eye is immediately attracted towards this subsidiary feature, which suggests – but does not prove – that its presence may have resulted from pressure by Gould, a lover of bright colours and gratuitous details.

Gratuitous or not, it provided an opportunity for Wolf to display his intimate knowledge of the details of bird structure. He told A.H. Palmer that very few people could tell at a glance the right foot of a bird from the left, if detached from the body. He provided Palmer with a ready method of distinguishing the one from the other. "The inner toe has one joint only," he said, "the one next the tarsus without the nail. The middle toe has two joints and the nail; the outer toe has one more. And with regard to the claws, particularly with Birds of Prey, the inner toe has a claw as strong as the claw on the hind toe. These two toes meet in clutching." Only someone who had spent many hours closely scrutinizing and sketching such objects could have made so assured an observation as this. Palmer, who, like most people, had probably never given a moment's thought to the structure of a bird's foot, was suitably impressed.

FALCO SACER.

Lanner Falcon (1868)

LANNER FALCON, *Falco lanarius (now Falco biarmicus)*. Hand-coloured litho-graph by H.C. Richter from an original drawing by J. Wolf, pl. 6 (in Part 28, 1868) from Vol. 1 of J. Gould's *The Birds of Asia*, 1849–83. Size of plate 21½″ × 14½″.

This small falcon occurs over most of Africa and in those countries bordering the north-eastern Mediterranean. Its plumage varies accord-ing to the region it inhabits and it is sometimes confused with the Peregrine. The Lanner frequenting Egypt and northern Africa is generally paler above, its underparts more spotted than barred. In the southern part of its range its plumage, towards the end of its life, is generally reddish.

"No region is too desolate or dreary for this noble bird," says Gould, and indeed the Lanner is essentially a bird of the open country and desert. Gould was wrong, however, in thinking that it avoids forests; it habitually penetrates far into them. When not soaring over hills or perching on a jutting rock or a tree, it is hunting for small mammals and reptiles on the ground, which it does rather expertly, or chasing birds or bats through the air, which it does with less mastery than the Peregrine.

Peregrine (c. 1844)

LE FAUCON HAGARD (Peregrine, *Falco peregrinus*). Hand-coloured lithograph by J. Wolf, with additional details by C. Scheuren, pl. 7 (c. 1844) from H. Schlegel and H.A. Verster van Wulverhorst's *Traité de Fauconnerie*, 1844–53. Size of plate 26½″ × 19½″.

The bird in this picture looks rather stiff and formal perched on its conventional branch, but this is not Wolf's fault. Most of his lithographs for the *Traité de Fauconnerie* were probably modelled upon mounted specimens set up by taxidermists who had not studied the birds in life. Collectively, however, they make up a superb gallery of portraits celebrating the delights of one of the oldest and most difficult of field sports. Eventually Wolf's pictures of Peregrines became unequalled for vivacity and truthfulness, the results of first-hand observation and artistic skill – and a passion for predatory birds.

Next to the Gyrfalcon, the Peregrine was the chosen bird of kings and other high-ranking personages, the different markings and colouring of each bird supposedly showing its degree of nobility and its hunting qualities. Like many other birds of prey, adult Peregrines do vary considerably in their plumage, but the variations do not suggest differences in hunting aptitude. Probably faster than any other falcon except the Gyrfalcon, the Peregrine is appreciated by falconers for its athleticism in the air and its ability to take a wide variety of game. Falconers prefer to hunt with the female because, as is usual among birds of prey, it is larger and stronger than the male. They also prefer to capture the Peregrine on its first migration and train it for service rather than train an inexperienced young bird taken from the eyrie. The adult caught in the wild is also used but may be difficult to handle. Such a bird, known as a haggard, is the subject of this picture.

Barbary Falcon (1868)

RED-NAPED FALCON, *Falco babylonicus* (now Barbary Falcon, *Falco pelegrinoides babylonicus*). Hand-coloured lithograph by H.C. Richter from an original drawing by J. Wolf, pl. 4 (in Part 20, 1868) from Vol. 1 of J. Gould's *The Birds of Asia*, 1849–83. Size of plate 21½″ × 14½″.

The Barbary Falcon, also known as the Shaheen, occurs across northern Africa, Arabia and westwards to Mongolia. It resembles the Peregrine in size and habits, but it is not blackish about the head and its plumage is generally paler. In North Africa and Arabia it has an amber-brown collar, but in the Asian form – shown here – it has a dark-brown collar and crown.

It winters in Pakistan and north-western India and would have been a familiar sight to British soldiers defending the Khyber Pass during the nineteenth century. Gould refers to an account of this bird's hunting ability by Major E.D. Radcliffe, who had observed it in the Himalayas. Certain breeding pairs were well known to the native chiefs who would regularly obtain young birds to train every year. Docile and good-tempered in training, the Barbary Falcon performed well in hilly country but less satisfactorily on the plains of India. Because of the very short hawking season, a lowland falconer who bought a bird bred in the mountains had difficulty in training and flying it satisfactorily in a short time.

Merlin (1865)

MERLIN, *Falco aesalon (now Falco columbarius)*. Hand-coloured lithograph by H.C. Richter from an original drawing by J. Wolf, pl. 19 (in Part 7, 1865) from Vol. 1 of J. Gould's *The Birds of Great Britain*, 1862–73. Size of plate 21¾″ × 14½″.

The Merlin, also known as the Pigeon Hawk in North America, is one of the smaller falcons, the female attaining a length of about twelve inches, the male not exceeding nine. Widely distributed in the colder regions of the northern hemisphere, its plumage varies between the sexes, the slate-blue upper parts of the male bird shown in the top half of Wolf's picture contrasting noticeably with the dark, greyish-brown of the female shown below. It also varies from region to region, birds from Vancouver in British Columbia being so dark that they are called "Black Pigeon Hawks". In the Old World it flies fast and hunts low over open country, feeding mostly upon small birds, which it pounces upon from a rapid flight. Even birds the size of pigeons are not safe from attack by this bold and adventurous falcon, and it creates havoc among shore birds such as sandpipers when it visits the coast.

Having given some chilling statistics in his *History of European Birds* about the destruction of Merlins and their nests in Britain during the 1870s, H.E. Dresser says: "The gamekeepers have found out by experience that it is no use to shoot the birds before they have begun to breed, as they so easily replace the loss. They shoot or snare the cock bird as soon as they can after the hen has begun to sit. In the neighbourhood of the nest are little rocky elevations on the ground which the cock uses as feeding-places, and which are easily found by the feathers of Meadow-pipits, Linnets, young Grouse etc. scattered around them. Upon these knolls traps are set. As soon as the cock bird is caught, the hen is easily shot off the nest." Very likely such barbarous acts ended the lives of the birds portrayed here.

FALCO ÆSALON, Linn.

J. Gould and H. C. Richter, del et lith.   Walter, Imp.

Hobby (1865)

HOBBY, *Falco subbuteo*. Hand-coloured lithograph by H.C. Richter from an original drawing by J. Wolf, pl. 18 (in Part 8, 1865) from Vol. 1 of J. Gould's *The Birds of Great Britain*, 1862–73. Size of plate 21¾″ × 14½″.

This exquisite study shows an adult male Hobby with a dragonfly held fast in its claws. The Hobby feeds mostly on large insects, especially dragonflies, but it will take birds when it is breeding and migrating. It is about the same size as the Merlin and is partial to swifts, swallows, martins and even bats, which its speed and agility enable it to snatch out of the air. Distributed across Europe and Asia, the Hobby has a fragile presence at the north-western limit of its range in southern England.

"If an ornithologist were requested to name the most elegant species of Falcon inhabiting the British Islands," says Gould, "he would unquestionably reply, the Hobby; for the proportions of no other raptorial bird are more evenly balanced, or the colours more harmoniously distributed." It seems as though the slender-winged and short-tailed Hobby was a favourite with Joseph Wolf himself. The Zoological Society of London has a portrait of the artist, painted in oils by Lance Calkin in 1890 (reproduced on the title-page of this book). Originally the painting showed Wolf with a cigar in his right hand, but he substituted for it a Hobby, a gesture suitably commemorating his attachment to predatory birds in general and, presumably, to the Hobby in particular.

Eastern Red-footed Falcon (1868)

ERYTHROPUS AMURENSIS (now Eastern Red-footed Falcon, *Falco amurensis*). Hand-coloured lithograph by J. Wolf, pl. 2 from *Ibis* (New Series), Vol. 4, 1868, illustrating an article by J.H. Gurney, "An eighth additional list of birds from Natal". Size of plate 8½" × 5".

Thomas Ayres sent three specimens of this species to J.H. Gurney with other bird skins he had obtained in Natal. "Numbers of these pretty Falcons may be seen during the summer months about the open downs in the neighbourhood of Maritzburg," says Ayres in his accompanying notes, "but are not (so far as I know) found there in winter. They hunt in company, sometimes as many as twenty together, well scanning the ground for grasshoppers and other insects, of which their food seems almost entirely to consist. They do not generally remain long on the wing, alighting on any low plant, ant-heap, or on the level ground, in twos and threes. They are not particularly shy; one may get within fifty yards of them without much difficulty. They seem to prefer marshy ground to hunt over." It was not known then that this bird of eastern Asia wintered predominantly in southern Africa, but Gurney was able to compare the specimens he had received with specimens from elsewhere in southern Africa and China. The comparison proved to him that he was dealing with only one species.

It is now widely agreed that this species is distinct from the Western Red-footed Falcon, *Falco vespertinus*, a bird widespread over the Soviet Union which winters predominantly in Angola, Botswana, Zimbabwe, Zambia and South Africa. It, too, feeds on swarms of locusts and other flying insects. Ornithologists still differ about the relationships of these two species, so similar in their appearance and habits.

J. Wolf lith.

M & N Hanhart imp

ERYTHROPUS AMURENSIS

Old World Kestrel (1862)

KESTREL, *Tinnunculus alaudarius* (now Old World Kestrel, *Falco tinnunculus*). Hand-coloured lithograph by H.C. Richter from an original drawing by J. Wolf, pl. 21 (in Part 2, 1862) from Vol. 1 of J. Gould's *The Birds of Great Britain*, 1862–73. Size of plate 21¾″ × 14½″.

Over most of its range there can be few predatory birds more familiar than the Old World Kestrel. Sometimes known as the Windhover in allusion to its habit of hovering conspicuously over open spaces, or these days over motorway verges, this distinctive falcon occurs throughout Europe, Asia and parts of Africa. Throughout its range it varies in size from eleven to nearly fourteen inches in length, the smallest specimens occurring on islands and the largest in eastern Siberia. It varies in colour too, European specimens being lighter than most others. The male's slate-blue head and tail distinguish it from the female everywhere except in western, central and southern Africa, where both sexes share these features.

The comparative abundance of this bird may be attributed, in part, to its wary tolerance of the human race. An illustration of this tolerance is given by Gould, who quotes from the observations of the Revd. H. H. Crewe, whose children caught a young male bird which became attached to them. Three years later it was still around. It would come every day to the nursery window and would enter the room and perch upon the chairs or table and sometimes upon the heads of the little ones, who always had a little piece of meat for him. "The male never leaves us," says The Revd Crewe, "indeed he is so attached to the children, that if we leave home for a time he is seldom seen; but as soon as we return, and he hears the voices of his little friends calling him by name, he comes flying over the fields, squealing with joy to see them again."

TINNUNCULUS ALAUDARIUS.

Collared Scops Owl (1844)

Le Hibou Petit-duc à Demi Collier, *Otus semitorques* (now Collared Scops Owl, *Otus bakkamoena semitorques*). Hand-coloured lithograph by J. Wolf, pl. 8 (1844) from P.F. von Siebold's *Fauna Japonica, Description des Oiseaux*, 1844–50. Size of plate 15½″ × 11″.

It was difficult for Wolf to inject life into the drawings he prepared for P.F. von Siebold's volume on Japanese birds. Siebold's preserved specimens, probably few and in poor shape, belonged mostly to species the artist had not seen in the wild or in captivity and about which little was known in the 1840s. Nothing significant was known then about the race of the Collared Scops Owl portrayed by him in this plate. He shows it with one eye closed, a simple but effective way to enliven an otherwise stiff portrait. Siebold had six specimens before him when describing the bird, but none would have had so whimsical an appearance in death. Joseph Wolf's general knowledge of owls was such that he could safely assume that the Collared Scops Owl did habitually close one eye.

Owls have large eyes, occasionally larger than our own, set in a forward-facing position on the facial disk, which ensures them a considerable degree of binocular vision – a useful facility for creatures which hunt mostly in poor light. It is an entirely normal practice for them to close one eye from time to time.

The Collared Scops Owl, which is about ten inches long, occurs in the temperate forest areas of Japan, northern China and the Himalayas, westwards as far as Oman and southwards as far as Java. It nests in hollow trees, old buildings and in the deserted nests of other birds. The Ainu people of Japan venerate this bird and address it as "Dear Little Divinity".

Eagle Owl (1866)

EAGLE OWL, *Bubo maximus* (now *Bubo bubo*). Hand-coloured lithograph by H.C. Richter from an original drawing by J. Wolf, pl. 30 (in Part 9, 1866) from Vol. 1 of J. Gould's *The Birds of Great Britain*, 1862–73. Size of plate 21¾″ × 14½″.

The Eagle Owl impressed Gould. "If I were to indulge in a poetic vein while writing the history of this noble species, which stands at the head of all European owls," he says, "I might speak of its selection as the emblem of all that is wise and learned, or I might take up another strain and write upon its midnight voice, or upon its presence being regarded as an omen of death and other evil forebodings." Coming upon it unexpectedly in the wild and at close quarters may be a thrilling and possibly frightening experience, as those lucky enough to have done so will testify. It may seem curious, therefore, that Wolf chooses not to emphasize its size, its nobility and its emblematic qualities, preferring instead to let its nestlings steal the limelight in this picture. But his preference is understandable as no other Victorian bird artist displays a greater knowledge of nestlings.

Even in Gould's day this was a scarce bird. He never saw it in the wild himself but retails two or three accounts by others which show how difficult it was to obtain a sight of it even in Scandinavia, then its headquarters. A century later it had become even more difficult; and the Eagle Owl would probably have been extinct there by the end of the twentieth century but for determined efforts by conservationists to increase the number of breeding pairs in Sweden. Success crowned these efforts, although the local inhabitants were not easily persuaded to share their environment with increasing numbers of a large and admittedly intimidating bird. The successful reintroduction of the Eagle Owl into the wild, however, was made possible mostly by the bird itself. Like many other owls it flourishes in captivity but speedily learns how to adapt to natural conditions. With luck, this imposing bird should thrill and frighten us for many years to come.

Snowy Owl (1863)

SNOWY OWL, *Nyctea nivea* (now *Nyctea scandiaca*). Hand-coloured lithograph by H.C. Richter from an original drawing by J. Wolf, pl. 34 (in Part 4, 1863) from Vol. 1 of J. Gould's *The Birds of Great Britain*, 1862–73. Size of plate 21¾″ × 14½″.

The heavy build and predominantly white plumage of the Snowy Owl make it one of the most unmistakable and – to our eyes – one of the most impressive of the owls. Although smaller than the Eagle Owl, it is still a large bird and is one of the most powerful for its size of all birds. The lack of ear tufts accentuates the half-moon character of its large head from which its widely spaced, deep-set, yellow eyes peer out. Some observers consider that these eyes give the head more the appearance of a cat than of an owl. Circumpolar in its distribution, the Snowy Owl breeds on the tundras beyond the northern limit of trees. It is so wary of man, the traditional enemy, that an intruder seldom gets within a hundred yards of it.

In most years the Snowy Owl is rarely seen except by Eskimos, who regularly collect its eggs, and by others who live in Arctic solitude. But, when lemmings and hares are scarce, it may appear in large numbers to hunt much farther south, reaching Texas and Georgia in the United States, England and France in Europe, and Turkestan in Asia and the Japanese island of Honshu.

Joseph Wolf not only painted what he saw but could often convey its essence. For example, he has captured perfectly here the soft, downy appearance of the Snowy Owl's breast feathers. He told his biographer, A.H. Palmer, that people generally had no idea of the differences between various kinds of feathers. "For instance, an Owl's feather is a soft, fluffy thing, whilst a Falcon's is hard. One floats in the air, and another falls to the ground so that you can hear it. The tail of a Woodpecker is as stiff as a piece of whalebone. The feather of an Owl is a ghost – you can hear nothing."

NYCTEA NIVEA.

J.Wolf and H.C.Richter del. et lith.

Walter & Cohn Imp.

Little Owl (1867)

LITTLE OWL, *Athene noctua*. Hand-coloured lithograph by H.C. Richter from an original drawing by J. Wolf, pl. 37 (in Part 11, 1867) from Vol. 1 of J. Gould's *The Birds of Great Britain*, 1862–73. Size of plate 21¾″ × 14½″.

Compared with portraits of the Little Owl by some twentieth-century bird artists, this one seems to be whimsical – almost a caricature of the bird. It may be merely a revised version of one of Wolf's earliest (and least successful) bird portraits, published in the *Abbildungen der Vögel Europas* by Johann and Eduard Susemihl. In Wolf's defence, however, it should be said that this flat-headed, plump and short-tailed bird does look whimsical when compared with most other European owls. It may even look slightly ridiculous, especially when seen bobbing up and down on a perch, glaring fixedly at an intruder.

During the nineteenth century the Little Owl was a rarity in the English countryside, although it was a common sight in western Europe. Nowadays, it occurs widely in Britain and often perches on telegraph wires during daylight hours. It has a loud, ringing call-note, and Gould quotes a relevant passage from Jean Baptiste Bailly's *Ornithologie de la Savoie* (1853–4). "These cries, distinctly uttered in a strong voice during the shades of evening and in the stillness of the night," says Bailly, "cause great alarm to those persons who are weak enough to believe in ghosts." Bailly also says that "it has the habit of pursuing by night, and especially in the early morning, with loud cries all who may pass along the roads bordered with trees near the places in which it is searching for prey. I have several times been accompanied by this Owl along the pathways and fields when going out shooting in the autumn. Near Chambéry one followed me for half an hour, jumping from tree to tree, and from house to house. Two shots fired at it, at random, did not prevent its following me; on the contrary, they caused it to redouble its cries; and in an instant afterwards I found myself accompanied by two others, which had doubtless been attracted thereby."

ATHENE NOCTUA.

Black-and-white Owl (1859)

CICCABA NIGROLINEATA (Black-and-white Owl, *Ciccaba nigrolineata*). Hand-coloured lithograph by J. Wolf, pl. 63 (1859) from *Transactions of the Zoological Society of London*, Vol. 4, 1851–62, illustrating an article by P.L. Sclater, "Description of a new species of Owl of the Genus *Ciccaba*." Size of plate 12″ × 9″.

Represented on this plate and the next are owls of the genus *Ciccaba*, sometimes known as "wood owls". Except for a single African species, the genus occurs only in Central and South America. When P.L. Sclater first saw a specimen of the bird portrayed here, now known as the Black-and-white Owl, he considered it to be the same as the Black-banded Owl, *Ciccaba huhula*; but he changed his mind after examining a second specimen. John Gurney acquired the first specimen for the Norwich Museum; and Wolf provided this lithograph of it to accompany Sclater's article describing *Ciccaba nigrolineata* as a new species. The two species differ in appearance and their ranges do not overlap, the Black-and-white Owl being a Central American bird, the Black-banded Owl occurring over a large part of north-eastern South America.

Like other *Ciccaba* species, the Black-and-white Owl has an average length of thirteen inches, a round face with distinct eyebrows and fine white bars on the sides of the neck. It frequents forest borders and tends to perch motionless on tree branches during the day. A night hunter, its diet consists mostly of large insects.

CICCABA NIGRO-LINEATA.

Rufous-banded Owl (1859)

SYRNIUM ALBITARSE (now Rufous-banded Owl, *Ciccaba albitarsus*). Hand-coloured lithograph by J. Wolf, pl. 60 (1859) from *Transactions of the Zoological Society of London*, Vol. 4, 1851–62, illustrating an article by P.L. Sclater, "On some new or little-known species of Accipitres, in the collection of the Norwich Museum". Size of plate 12″ × 9″.

It is easy to forget that our accumulated knowledge of birds of the world has been hard won. Ornithologists may now concentrate on filling in the gaps in that knowledge which largely concerns bird behaviour. In the nineteenth century, however, one of the main occupations of ornithologists was to describe birds previously unknown or poorly understood. Sometimes they had to reach conclusions from the study of only one or two dead skins. Time after time Wolf had to provide lifelike illustrations based upon those same skins. When illustrating the Rufous-banded Owl for P.L. Sclater, for instance, he had only one skin to work from. It is almost certain, however, that he could match Sclater's knowledge of living birds and so could reconstruct its probable appearance in life.

As this owl occurs in humid forests on the slopes of the Andes, from Venezuela to Ecuador, it was some time before additional specimens became available. Slightly smaller and lighter coloured than the Black-and-white Owl, its life history may differ only in minor respects from that of other *Ciccaba* species.

Tawny Owl (1864)

TAWNY OR BROWN OWL, *Syrnium aluco* (now Tawny Owl). Hand-coloured lithograph by H.C. Richter from an original drawing by J. Wolf, pl. 29 (in Part 5, 1864) from Vol. 1 of J. Gould's *The Birds of Great Britain*, 1862–73. Size of plate 21¾″ × 14½″.

In Britain and parts of mainland Europe this is the familiar black-eyed, brown-faced owl perched on an urban lamp-post being mobbed by smaller birds, the *tu-whit-tu-whoo* owl which haunted our childhood and still colours our literature. The Tawny Owl, for many of us, is the quintessential owl. Originally a woodland bird, Wolf pictures it in a mature tree with a cavity as a nesting site, still its preferred home. By the end of the nineteenth century, however, indiscriminate gamekeeping had destroyed so many Tawny Owls that they had become very scarce, in Britain anyway. In the first half of the twentieth century their numbers increased considerably and they began to move into cemeteries, parks and other suburban enclaves where they are now familiar and accepted residents.

To survive in its new environment the Tawny Owl had to change its eating habits. As well as the rodents and other small mammals which used to constitute most of its diet, it has learned to catch town birds, especially sparrows and pigeons, and sometimes it will prey on such birds almost exclusively. Bird-catching is not a recent accomplishment of this owl, however, for, as Gould says, "its prowling habit leads it to pounce, during the stillness of the night, upon sleeping Blackbirds, Thrushes, or any other species it can master." Gould also says, "strange as it may appear, it also hunts the edges of pools and rivers and captures living fish," and he quotes several instances of this unlikely behaviour to show that the Tawny Owl is a skilled fisherman. Not surprisingly, this versatile and adaptable owl is widely distributed, occupying a broad band from western Europe to south-eastern China.

Great Grey Owl (1879)

LAPP OWL, *Syrnium lapponicum* (now Great Grey Owl, *Strix nebulosa*). Hand-coloured lithograph by W. Hart from an original drawing by J. Wolf, pl. 308 (in Parts 73–4, 1879) from Vol. 5 of H. E. Dresser's *A History of the Birds of Europe*, 1871–96. Size of plate 12″ × 9½″.

This imposing bird, about as large as the Eagle Owl, occurs from Scandinavia across northern Europe and Asia as far as Korea. It is also widely distributed across the northern part of North America – the only member of its genus to be present in the New World and the Old. North American examples are larger, darker in colour and more heavily barred on the belly than their Old World cousins. The facial disc, so striking a feature of the bird in the foreground of Wolf's picture, provides an extraordinary setting for the small, yellow eyes and immediately distinguishes this owl from any other. The voluminous feathers make it seem larger than it is, but their main function is to insulate it from the cold. It frequents the "taiga", a moist, subarctic belt of forest dominated by spruce and fir. There its greyish colouring enables it to blend into its surroundings, especially when it perches on a moss-laden branch. When it moves among human establishments, such as farms, it becomes more conspicuous.

Great Grey Owls living in the far north must hunt during the perpetual daylight of the Arctic summer, making them the only truly diurnal members of the genus *Strix*, those from farther south becoming more truly nocturnal in their habits. Normally they prey almost exclusively upon voles, but when these are scarce the hungry birds fly south to more favourable hunting-grounds. Their invasions into Europe usually coincide with shortages of voles in northern Russia.

$\frac{1}{3}$

J.Wolf del.
W.Hart lith.

LAPP-OWL.

SYRNIUM LAPPONICUM.

Long-eared Owl (1863)

LONG-EARED OWL, *Otus vulgaris* (now *Asio otus*). Hand-coloured lithograph by H.C. Richter from an original drawing by J. Wolf, pl. 31 (in Part 4, 1863) from Vol. 1 of J. Gould's *The Birds of Great Britain*, 1862–73. Size of plate 21¾″ × 14½″.

The Old World form of the Long-eared Owl, portrayed here, occurs right across temperate Europe and central Asia as far as Japan. It differs from the New World form, which occupies most of central North America, by being generally lighter in colour and by having less prominent streaks and bars on the breast and underparts. The elongated face and long ear tufts of this shy and furtive bird help to accentuate its slim outline. Contrary to appearances the ear tufts of owls have nothing to do with their ears; they are merely elongated feathers which seem to help the owls recognize each other. The true ears are just behind the eyes and are covered by ear flaps corresponding to the outer edges of the facial disk.

The Long-eared Owl is essentially a woodland species. In Europe it prefers coniferous woods, where it seldom encounters its stronger rival the Tawny Owl, but it will also frequent other woods, plantations and isolated trees. Throughout its range it preys on rodents, with voles and mice providing most of its food in the Old World, mice and gophers providing most of it in the New World, and with diminutive birds making up a small percentage of the total. Here Wolf situates the nest in a coniferous tree, a likely place for it, although the Long-eared Owl usually adopts one abandoned by another kind of bird. A mature tree is not its obligatory nesting site; sometimes it makes a nest on the ground. Once again Joseph Wolf displays his sound knowledge of nestlings, their inclusion here adding to the interest of the picture and helping to balance its composition.

OTUS VULGARIS.

J.Wolf and H.C.Richter, del et lith.

Walter & Cohn, Imp.

INDEX